The Laws of the Knowledge Workplace

Reviews for
The Laws of the Knowledge Workplace: Changing Roles and the Meaning of Work in Knowledge-Intensive Environments

The Laws of the Knowledge Workplace *is not just another publication on a fashionable topic. It goes beyond the easy introduction of the "knowledge work" and "knowledge workers" concepts. The authors dig deeper, and in research-based chapters introduce work as perceived by the knowledge workers themselves. It focuses on the ways knowledge workers define, organize and make sense of their workplace. Moreover, it presents studies from different cultural contexts, and this international perspective is still insufficiently researched and described. In my opinion this book is critical reading for anyone who wants to understand the nature, and multidimensional character of knowledge work.*

Beata Glinka, The University of Warsaw, Poland

Knowledge workers are praised as the most value-adding group of employees, and analyzed as gurus, hired guns or warm bodies. Their diploma-wielding and cappuccino-sipping clusters advance business companies to the ranks of knowledge-intensive organizations. But do we really know what knowledge workers do when they work? Jemielniak and his authors decided to listen to their stories. Do they enjoy a chance to be creative or deplore a collapse of a distinction between work and household time? What are the managerial lingos and employee power games between clouded onliners, the wizards of the world wide web, who trust but check? Virtual teams and virtual organizing are studied along with nepotism and networking, trust and professional identities, power and roles. Speaking of the laws of knowledge work betrays ambition to go beyond the functional, neopositivist paradigm of quantitatively biased mainstream research projects. Harvard's labor and worklife program and Kozminski's university sabbatical are among the "establishment" sponsors of this mildly subversive but strongly recommended collection of studies. All of them confirm that "innovation becomes increasingly a collective game" and that network leadership is one of the safer bets on desirable futures (Czakon and Klimas on the growth of Polish Aviation Valley's professional networks). Reality check? Yes, please.

Slawomir Magala, Rotterdam School of Management and Kozminski University, Poland

The Laws of the Knowledge Workplace

Changing Roles and the Meaning of Work in Knowledge-Intensive Environments

Edited by
DARIUSZ JEMIELNIAK
Kozminski University, Poland

GOWER

© Dariusz Jemielniak 2014

All rights reserved. No part of this publication may be reproduced, stored in a retrieval system or transmitted in any form or by any means, electronic, mechanical, photocopying, recording or otherwise without the prior permission of the publisher.

Dariusz Jemielniak has asserted his right under the Copyright, Designs and Patents Act, 1988, to be identified as the editor of this work.

Gower Applied Business Research
Our programme provides leaders, practitioners, scholars and researchers with thought provoking, cutting edge books that combine conceptual insights, interdisciplinary rigour and practical relevance in key areas of business and management.

Published by
Gower Publishing Limited
Wey Court East
Union Road
Farnham
Surrey, GU9 7PT
England

Gower Publishing Company
110 Cherry Street
Suite 3-1
Burlington, VT 05401-3818
USA

www.gowerpublishing.com

British Library Cataloguing in Publication Data
A catalogue record for this book is available from the British Library

ISBN: 978 1 4724 2388 7 (hbk)
ISBN: 978 1 4724 2389 4 (ebk – ePDF)
ISBN: 978 1 4724 2390 0 (ebk – ePUB)

Library of Congress Cataloging-in-Publication Data
The laws of the knowledge workplace : changing roles and the meaning of work in knowledge-intensive environments / by Dariusz Jemielniak.
  pages cm
 Includes bibliographical references and index.
 ISBN 978-1-4724-2388-7 (hbk) -- ISBN 978-1-4724-2389-4 (ebook) -- ISBN 978-1-4724-2390-0 (epub) 1. Knowledge workers. 2. Work environment. 3. Facility management. 4. Management. 5. Burn out (Psychology) I. Jemielniak, Dariusz, editor of compilation.
 HD8039.K59L397 2014
 658.4'038--dc23

2014008389

Printed in the United Kingdom by Henry Ling Limited, at the Dorset Press, Dorchester, DT1 1HD

Contents

List of Figures and Tables   *vii*
About the Editor   *ix*
About the Contributors   *xi*

1   Introducing the Laws of the Knowledge Workplace   1
     Dariusz Jemielniak

2   Accretion, Angst and Antidote: The Transition from Knowledge Worker to Manager in the UK Heritage Sector in an Era of Austerity   11
     Alistair Bowden and Malgorzata Ciesielska

3   Nepotism and Turnover Intentions amongst Knowledge Workers in Saudi Arabia   25
     Maryam Alhamadi Aldossari and Dorota Joanna Bourne

4   Knowledge Work and the Problem of Implementation: The Case of Engineering   35
     Lars Bo Henriksen

5   Coordinating the Repair and Modification of Offshore Production Systems: The Role of the Project Manager   55
     Vidar Hepsø

6   Role of the Virtual Team Leader: Managing Changing Membership in a Team   79
     Kaja Prystupa-Rządca and Dominika Latusek-Jurczak

7   Decision Support Systems as Knowledge Workers   97
     Aleksandra Przegalińska

8   Qualitative Research on the Organization of Work in Internet Prosumer Projects   113
     Sebastian Skolik

9   Innovative Networks in Knowledge-Intensive Industries: How
    to Make Them Work? An Empirical Investigation into the Polish
    Aviation Valley   133
    Wojciech Czakon and Patrycja Klimas

Index   *159*

List of Figures and Tables

Figures

5.1	Subsea production systems on the seabed	60
6.1	Role of the leader in virtual teams	81
7.1	Knowledge acquisition	105
7.2	Sender and recipient	105
7.3	Input to output	106
7.4	Category selecting	108
9.1	Aviation Valley Association network growth	145

Tables

9.1	Features and functions of a network-leading entity	136
9.2	Components of a network key actor's role	138
9.3	Projects conducted via Aviation Valley	147
9.4	Functions of the AVA's key actors	148

About the Editor

Dr Dariusz Jemielniak is an associate professor of management and head of the Center for Research on Organizations and Workplaces (CROW) at Kozminski University in Warsaw, Poland.

After completing his PhD at Kozminski University, Jemielniak spent a year as a Fulbright Scholar at Cornell University in the USA. He was then appointed as an assistant professor of management back at Kozminski University. He spent two semesters as a visiting scholar to Harvard University and at the University of California, Berkeley.

Completing his habilitation, he became an associate professor and then spent a year at Harvard Law School, undertaking projects on lawyers' workplace enactment and Wikipedic organizational culture. Dr Jemielniak's current research interests revolve around critical management studies, open collaboration projects, narrativity, storytelling, knowledge-intensive organizations, virtual communities and organizational archetypes.

The Center for Research on Organizations and Workplaces was founded at Kozminski University in 2009 and Dr Jemielniak was appointed as its head. He is already widely published and is author of *The New Knowledge Workers*, published by Edward Elgar in 2012.

About the Contributors

Maryam Alhamadi Aldossari is a PhD researcher at the School of Business and Management at Queen Mary University of London. Her research interest is in the effect of national and organizational culture on the repatriation process and human resource management (HRM) practices in general. The focus of her PhD research is on the effects of repatriation on the psychological contract in the Saudi Arabian context. Maryam has also conducted research on Saudi women working in Saudi Arabia. Her research focuses on the problems they encountered in Saudi society: a constitution and legal system that sanctions male superiority, and segregation of sexes in all areas.

Dorota Joanna Bourne works as a lecturer in organizational behaviour at the School of Business and Management at Queen Mary University of London. Her work is international, interdisciplinary and comparative in nature. She undertakes applied and practice-oriented research projects, such as the creation of spin-off companies, the implementation of organizational change programmes and the development of new HRM tools and techniques. Dorota combines various research methods in her work, which include ethnographic methodology and narrative methods in conjunction with tools derived from Personal Construct Psychology (PCP). Her current work involves the deepening of her research on HRM, management of change and organizational learning as well as the widening of her methodological contribution involving repertory grid-based research.

Alistair Bowden is a PhD student at Teesside University, researching the nature of strategy in hybrid organizations. He is interested in complexity and emergence, parallels between social systems and the natural world, and different perspectives on time and place. He was awarded an MBA from the University of Durham, where he won a prize for best dissertation and published his research on distributed innovation and knowledge management. Prior to this his academic background was in geology, carrying out research in palaeontology and stratigraphy. He has worked as a museum curator, heritage manager and freelance consultant, and has published widely in academic, practitioner and popular literature.

Malgorzata Ciesielska is a senior lecturer in organizational behaviour and HRM at Teesside University. She holds a PhD in organization and management studies from Copenhagen Business School, a first-class MSc in business management and a marketing degree from Warsaw University, Poland. Her research interests range from digital economy and innovation to gender and HRM in high-tech industries. She specializes in qualitative research methods. Her recent publications include an analysis of trust in open source software projects (*Tamara Journal for Critical Organization Inquiry*, 2013) and challenges for open source businesses (*Journal of Organizational Change Management*, forthcoming).

Wojciech Czakon is a professor at the Faculty of Management at the University of Economics in Katowice, and head of the Management Theory Department. His research revolves around inter-organizational phenomena, structures, processes and strategies. He uses both qualitative and quantitative methods, with a strong preference for in-depth case studies. His recent publications focus on competition strategies, social capital impact on competitive advantage and networks on strategies in various empirical settings, ranging from high-tech industries to tourism. He is also co-chair of the Doctoral Colloquium run by the European Academy of Management.

Lars Bo Henriksen works as a professor in engineering practice and engineering education at the Department of Planning, Aalborg University, Denmark. His work is mainly concerned with engineers' everyday life and the education of engineers in a problem-based learning (PBL) context. Lars Bo's research is mainly based on hermeneutic philosophies, ethnographic and practice-oriented research methods – always conducted in close contact with practitioners in the field, be they engineers in industry or educators in engineering schools. His current work involves studies in engineering practice and engineers' role as managers and facilitators of change projects.

Vidar Hepsø is an adjunct professor at the Norwegian University of Science and Technology (NTNU) in Trondheim. His PhD is in anthropology and science/technology studies. Most of his research is on new ways of working in organizations enabled by new information and communication technologies. His interests also include socio-technical approaches to the studies of technology development and innovation more in general. He is affiliated with the Center for Integrated Operations in the Oil Industry at NTNU and also works as a researcher in a Norwegian oil company.

Patrycja Klimas is assistant professor at the University of Economics in Katowice. Her research interests focus on inter-organizational cooperation, competition, networking and innovativeness. Her research projects are related to high-tech and creative industries, namely the aviation and video game sectors. She uses both qualitative and quantitative research methods while specializing in multivariate regression and social network analysis. However, her latest methodological interests refer to the application of structural equation modelling. Patrycja's recent publications include innovation networks, organizational innovativeness, organizational proximity and interpersonal relationships within networks.

Dominika Latusek-Jurczak is an associate professor at Kozminski Business School. Her research interests include inter-organizational collaboration, trust and high-tech industries. She was a Fulbright Scholar at Stanford University, where she conducted fieldwork on Silicon Valley companies.

Kaja Prystupa-Rządca is a research assistant in the Management Department at Kozminski University. Her research interests include knowledge management, innovativeness and virtual environments. Her recent research project was devoted to knowledge management in born-global companies from the example of the game production industry.

Aleksandra Przegalińska is an assistant professor at Kozminski University. A member of the Center for Research on Organizations and Workplaces and the European Network for Social Intelligence (Sintelnet), she holds a PhD in philosophy and is a graduate of philosophy and journalism and communication studies at the University of Wroclaw, as well as interdisciplinary studies in the humanities at the Liberales Artes Academy. As a Fulbright Scholar, Dr Przegalińska majored in sociology at the New School for Social Research in New York, where she participated in research on identity in virtual reality, with particular emphasis on second life. She is primarily interested in transhumanism and the consequences of introducing artificial beings and systems into people's social and professional spheres.

Sebastian Skolik is an assistant professor at the Technical University of Częstochowa. His research interests focus on free culture movement, open collaboration projects and institutionalization processes in online social spaces. He uses both qualitative and quantitative research methods, mainly case studies and content analysis. His recent publications focus on the evolution of prosumption, intellectual and social capital in online projects, relationships between copyright and freedom of speech in the Internet environment – interpersonal relationships in Wikimedia communities.

Chapter 1
Introducing the Laws of the Knowledge Workplace

DARIUSZ JEMIELNIAK

The Laws of the Knowledge Workplace is a project resulting from a research grant from the Polish National Science Center,[1] and was possible thanks to a generous visiting study offer from Harvard University (the Labor and Worklife Program) and a sabbatical granted by Kozminski University.

The book collects research-based chapters on knowledge workers. By presenting accounts and studies from management, organization studies, sociology, and anthropology of work it allows us to gain a deeper, interdisciplinary insight into qualitative studies of knowledge professions. In particular, it covers the issues of professional identity, time overruns, symbolic sacrifices in work, and burn-out, and studies the preferred as well as the disfavoured managerial practices in knowledge-intensive companies.

The project is purposely interdisciplinary: it blends study foci from anthropology, sociology, management, and administrative sciences. In particular, the methods involved are also those not coming from the functional paradigm currently dominant in management (Pfeffer, 1993, 1995; Van Maanen, 1995a, 1995b).

The aim of the book is to collect research-based chapters on the notion of power, management, identity, trust, play, family, and scheduling as perceived by the knowledge workers themselves. This view is certainly slightly skewed by stereotypes of this occupation (Gill, 2003). Still, even stereotypes manifest the ways in which organizational reality is constructed; they are actually job identity expressions, too. They are nothing more, but also nothing less than a particular kind of stories by which actors organize and make sense of their

---

1   Grant agreement no. 4116/B/H03/2011/40.

workplace (Boje, 1991; Feldman and Skölberg, 2004). Professional roles are socially constructed, enacted, and articulated in discourse and symbols (Berger and Luckman, 1967; Weick, 1969/79; Barley, 1983). In this light the things that members of the analyzed group say form reenactments of their roles. By describing their view on schedules, structures, power, trust, management, organizations, workplace, etc., the employees reproduce the sense and artefacts of daily work (Czarniawska-Joerges, 1992; Krzyworzeka, 2008) and form the basis for their identity and ideology (Czarniawska-Joerges, 1988). Therefore the interest of the collected volume is focused on understanding and interpreting what the studied knowledge workers say and mean, what the important topics of their everyday conversations are, or what the categorizations they make in sense-making their work are, and not on whether they are right or wrong, fair or biased.

Knowledge workers are, at least officially, considered to be the most important group in modern organizations. The popularity of this discourse in the official organizational language and literature leads to an interesting paradox: on one hand knowledge workers are perceived as the most valued members of organizations; they are endowed with "professional" status like medics in the old times (Hall, 1986; Abbott, 1988; Brante, 1988), and their professional knowledge serves as a source of new organizational power and recognition (Brint, 1994). On the other hand, they are being manipulated and "engineered", commonly driven to burn-out, and deprived of a private life (Kunda, 1992; Perlow, 2003; Styhre, 2013). Such a discrepancy between the official bureaucratic "rational" language and the actual practice is by no means new (Höpfl, 1995; Grant et al., 1998; Knights and Willmott, 1999), but in the case of knowledge-intensive companies, such as legal firms or software houses, is particularly visible. Moreover, it is concurrent with very specifically developed occupational cultures (Kraft, 1977; Bucciarelli, 1988; Trice and Beyer, 1993; Garsten, 1994; Kunda and Van Maanen, 1999; Hertzum, 2002; Vallas, 2003; Kunda and Ailon-Souday, 2005; Koźmiński et al., 2009). Manager–worker conflict is taken to a different level (Rosen, 1991; Van Maanen, 1991; Martin, 1993; Roscigno and Hodson, 2004). Maybe this is why the symbolic sacrifices for organizations are so demanded. Although depicted as "rational", they still play a very ritualistic role, and include ostentatious time dedication, giving up gender, resigning from family, etc. (Czarniawska-Joerges and Höpfl, 2002; Jacobs and Gerson, 2004; Jemielniak, 2009). As a result, the distinctions between work and household time are blurred and no longer limited physically (Hochschild, 1997). All this leads to significant changes in modern knowledge-intensive workplaces all around the world. The new economy of organizational relations emerges along with shifts in organizational power (Foucault, 1982; Latour, 1986).

The changes in occupational roles (including managerial ones), especially in knowledge-intensive environments, are by no means small. In fact, the meaning of work has been undergoing serious changes over the last 20 years. Its organization has evolved from the traditional industrial-bureaucratic model in which the standardization of work processes, planning, structural design, control, and formalization are most important (Mintzberg, 1993). As a result, identity-shaping, indoctrination, and creation of emotions become parts of managers' routines (Jackall, 1988; Kärreman and Alvesson, 2004). The evaluation of an employee's work becomes more dependent on his/her intentions and loyalty than just the result.

This phenomenon is still yet insufficiently researched and described, especially from an international perspective. Although many studies have delved into the issue of particular organizations or national changes in labour, there are virtually no qualitative researchers analyzing the shifts in modern work across nations, and in particular studying best practices in knowledge work from the point of view of the worker. This is a significant gap in the scholarship that calls for furthering. This topic, however, is of the utmost significance for management science and also for understanding knowledge-intensive organizations' competitiveness. Thus, the present volume aims at studying the enactment of the workplace in knowledge-intensive organizations. The goal of the project is to research the "interpretive community" of knowledge workers, their perceptions of work, organizations, management, schedules, family and authority.

Even though managerial literature often points to, and even recommends, an egalitarian and democratic approach to that group of employees (Horibe, 1999; Amar, 2002; Newell et al., 2002), other research findings attest that the reality of work in knowledge-intensive (K-I) organizations is quite different (Kunda, 1992; Hochschild, 1997; Perlow, 2003). The contributors to this edited volume try to address the paradox of rhetorical ambivalence present in many knowledge-intensive organizations.

The organizational and managerial practices in knowledge work are only beginning to be thoroughly delved into (Mosco and Stevens, 2007; Sveiby, 2007), and so far not from a qualitative and comparative perspective. Taking this into account, as well as the utmost importance of knowledge-intensive work in general economic and organizational development (Huggins and Izushi, 2007; Latusek and Jemielniak, 2007; Styhre, 2008) and the huge influence that organizational and occupational culture has on its effectiveness (Jemielniak, 2002; Davenport, 2005), it is clear that the topic is important.

Quite a lot of knowledge-intensive employees work for corporations. What motivates knowledge workers to work for corporations? How do they define creative aspects of their work? What do they like about their jobs? How do they perceive the organizations they work for: their managers, the schedules they are subject to? What is the understanding of timing in knowledge work, so often prone to delays? How does organizational culture differ in corporations successful in time-management from these that are less successful? What is the construction of power in knowledge-intensive environments? To what extent are the procedures and managerial lingo read as means of disempowerment? What are the factors influencing the professional status of a knowledge worker? How do knowledge workers enact trust and distrust in the workplace? Which factors determine knowledge worker occupational identity formation? What playful behaviors in the workplace are typical for knowledge workers? These questions are just a few examples of areas that the contributors to this volume found interesting. The structure of this volume is as follows.

Alistair Bowden and Malgorzata Ciesielska write about a fascinating shift from knowledge worker to manager in the UK heritage sector. The results of their longitudinal study allow them to make the point that although in current literature the model of advancement and development of a career is often presented, in fact the transition from a knowledge worker to someone who has to manage other knowledge workers' performance is much more profound and requires a redefinition of the social role.

Maryam Alhamadi Aldossari and Dorota Joanna Bourne address the problem of nepotism and turnover intentions among knowledge workers in Saudi Arabia. They refer to the problems faced by expats and repatriates. In the example of the Saudi Arabian private sector, they describe the issues of staff turnover as well as knowledge expansion in the context of governmental policy for international assignments and the cultural background of nepotism.

Lars Bo Henriksen also focuses on the actual practices of the knowledge-intensive workplace. He discusses the problems of implementation of engineering projects. He uses a storytelling method to present a fascinating narrative about the translation of ideas (rather than their diffusion) in engineering work. He uses actor-network theory to shed new light on what the education of knowledge workers should look like, and postulates a more holistic approach to the social, the discursive, and the technical aspects of knowledge work.

Vidar Hepsø studies engineers as well, but analyzes coordinating work issues in offshore production systems. He bases his chapter on a qualitative study of Norwegian oil industry. He studies the leader role enactment and the issues of trust and coordination of work in the kinds of knowledge work requiring closer coordination: the repair and modification of offshore production.

Kaja Prystupa-Rządca and Dominika Latusek-Jurczak address a very similar problem, but focus on virtual networks. They describe the role of the leader in virtual teams. Since virtual teams are an increasingly popular form of organization of work, the problems of managing them are of utmost importance for organization studies. Virtual teams are more conflict-driven, and their socialization is more difficult. Prystupa-Rządca and Latusek-Jurczak show that even though a life-cycle approach to product development in virtual teams is difficult, their leadership may benefit more from a dynamic approach to membership roles.

Staying in the virtual world, Aleksandra Przegalińska writes about decision support systems as knowledge workers. She presents a case-study of the Moral Knowledge Expert System, aimed at taking the moral impact of a decision into account of the algorithm. She aims to show the blurring boundaries between human and non-human actors serving as experts in knowledge management decision-making systems.

Sebastian Skolik continues the exploration of virtual organizing, and focuses on qualitative research on the organization of work in Internet prosumer projects. In the example of his fieldwork on Wikipedia, he presents the practical application of a new research method, netnography, as a possible tool for an analysis of the knowledge workplace.

In the last chapter, Wojciech Czakon and Patrycja Klimas describe the problem of making innovative networks work in knowledge-intensive industries. They study network leadership in the example of so-called "Aviation Valley", a region known for aviation industry development. They bring conclusions about new ways of gaining competitive advantage in knowledge-intensive companies: through network coordination, knowledge management, and relationship building.

References

Abbott, A.D. (1988). *The System of Professions: An Essay on the Division of Expert Labor*. Chicago, IL: University of Chicago Press.

Amar, A.D. (2002). *Managing Knowledge Workers: Unleashing Innovation and Productivity*. Westport, CT: Quorum.

Barley, S. (1983). Semantics and the study of occupational and organizational cultures. *Administrative Science Quarterly*, 28, 393–31.

Berger, P.L., and Luckman, T. (1967). *The Social Construction of Reality: A Treatise in the Sociology of Knowledge*. Garden City, NY: Doubleday.

Boje, D.M. (1991). The storytelling organization: A study of story performance in an office-supply firm. *Administrative Science Quarterly*, 36(1), 106–26.

Brante, T. (1988). Sociological approaches to the professions. *Acta Sociologica*, 31(2), 119–42.

Brint, S.G. (1994). *In an Age of Experts: The Changing Role of Professionals in Politics and Public Life*. Princeton, NJ: Princeton University Press.

Bucciarelli, L.L. (1988). An ethnographic perspective on engineering design. *Design Studies*, 9(3), 159–78.

Czarniawska-Joerges, B. (1988). *Ideological Control in Nonideological Organizations*. New York: Praeger.

Czarniawska-Joerges, B. (1992). *Exploring Complex Organizations: A Cultural Perspective*. Newbury Park, CA: Sage.

Czarniawska-Joerges, B., and Höpfl, H. (2002). *Casting the Other: The Production and Maintenance of Inequalities in Work Organizations*. London and New York: Routledge.

Davenport, T.H. (2005). *Thinking for a Living: How to Get Better Performance and Results from Knowledge Workers*. Boston, MA: Harvard Business School Press.

Feldman, M.S., and Skölberg, K. (2004). Stories and the rhetoric of contrariety: Subtexts of organizing (change). *Culture and Organization*, 8(4), 275–92.

Foucault, M. (1982). The subject and power. In H.L. Dreyfus and P. Rabinow (eds), *Michel Foucault: Beyond Structuralism and Hermeneutics*. Brighton: Harvester.

Garsten, C. (1994). *Apple World: Core and Periphery in a Transnational Organizational Culture*. Stockholm: Stockholm University Press.

Gill, M.J. (2003). Biased against "them" more than "him": Stereotype use in group-directed and individual-directed judgments. *Social Cognition*, 21(5), 321–48.

Grant, D., Keenoy, T., and Oswick, C. (1998). *Discourse and Organization*. London and Thousand Oaks, CA: Sage.

Hall, R.H. (1986). *Dimensions of Work*. Beverly Hills, CA: Sage.

Hertzum, M. (2002). The importance of trust in software engineers' assessment and choice of information sources. *Information and Organization*, 12, 1–12.

Hochschild, A.R. (1997). *The Time Bind: When Work Becomes Home and Home Becomes Work*. New York: Metropolitan.

Höpfl, H. (1995). Organizational rhetoric and the threat of ambivalence. *Studies in Cultures, Organizations and Societies*, 1(2), 175–87.

Horibe, F. (1999). *Managing Knowledge Workers: New skills and Attitudes to Unlock the Intellectual Capital in Your Organization*. Toronto and New York: Wiley.

Huggins, R., and Izushi, H. (2007). *Competing for Knowledge: Creating, Connecting, and Growing*. London and New York: Routledge.

Jackall, R. (1988). *Moral Mazes: The World of Corporate Managers*. New York: Oxford University Press.

Jacobs, J.A., and Gerson, K. (2004). *The Time Divide: Work, Family, and Gender Inequality*. Cambridge, MA: Harvard University Press.

Jemielniak, D. (2002). Kultura: odkrywana czy konstruowana? *Master of Business Administration*, 2(55), 28–30.

Jemielniak, D. (2009). Time as symbolic currency in knowledge work. *Information and Organization*, 19, 277–93.

Kärreman, D., and Alvesson, M. (2004). Cages in tandem: Management control, social identity, and identification in a knowledge-intensive firm. *Organization*, 11(1), 149–76.

Knights, D., and Willmott, H. (1999). *Management Lives: Power and Identity in Work Organizations*. London and Thousand Oaks, CA: Sage.

Koźmiński, A.K., Jemielniak, D., and Latusek, D. (2009). Współczesne spojrzenie na kulturę organizacji. *e-mentor*, 3(30), 4–13.

Kraft, P. (1977). *Programmers and Managers: The Routinization of Computer Programming in the United States*. New York: Springer-Verlag.

Krzyworzeka, P. (2008). Kultura i organizacje: Perspektywa antropologiczna. In M. Kostera (ed.), *Nowe kierunki w zarządzaniu*. Warsaw: Wydawnictwa Akademickie i Profesjonalne.

Kunda, G. (1992). *Engineering Culture: Control and Commitment in a High-Tech Corporation*. Philadelphia, PA: Temple University Press.

Kunda, G., and Ailon-Souday, G. (2005). Managers, markets, and ideologies: Design and devotion revisited. In S. Ackroyd, R.L. Batt, P. Thompson and P.S. Tolbert (eds), *The Oxford Handbook of Work and Organization*. Oxford: Oxford University Press.

Kunda, G., and Van Maanen, J. (1999). Changing scripts at work: Managers and professionals. *Annals of the American Academy of Political and Social Science*, 561(1), 64–80.

Latour, B. (1986). The powers of association. In J. Law (ed.), *Power, Action and Belief: A New Sociology of Knowledge?* London: Routledge and Kegan Paul.

Latusek, D., and Jemielniak, D. (2007). (Dis)trust in software projects: A thrice told tale. On dynamic relationships between software engineers, IT project managers, and customers. *International Journal of Technology, Knowledge and Society*, 3(1), 117–25.

Martin, J. (1993). *Cultures in Organizations: Three Perspectives*. New York: Oxford University Press.

Mintzberg, H. (1993). *Structure in Fives: Designing Effective Organizations*. Englewood Cliffs, NJ: Prentice-Hall.

Mosco, V., and Stevens, A. (2007). Outsourcing knowledge work: Labor responds to the new international division of labor. In C. McKercher and V. Mosco (eds), *Knowledge Workers in the Information Society*. Lanham, MD: Lexington.

Newell, S., Robertson, M., Scarbrough, H., and Swan, J. (2002). *Managing Knowledge Work*. New York: Palgrave.

Perlow, L.A. (2003). *When You Say Yes But Mean No: How Silencing Conflict Wrecks Relationships and Companies ... and What You Can Do About It*. New York: Crown Business.

Pfeffer, J. (1993). Barriers to the Advance of organizational science: Paradigm development as a dependent variable. *Academy of Management Review*, 18(4), 599–620.

Pfeffer, J. (1995). Mortality, reproducibility, and the persistence of styles of theory. *Organization Science*, 6(6), 681–6.

Roscigno, V.J., and Hodson, R. (2004). The organizational and social foundations of worker resistance. *American Sociological Review*, 69(1), 14–39.

Rosen, M. (1991). Breakfast at Spiro's: Dramaturgy and dominance. In P.J. Frost, L.F. Moore, M.R. Louis, C.C. Lundberg, and J. Martin (eds), *Reframing Organizational Culture*. Newbury Park, CA: Sage.

Styhre, A. (2008). *Science-Based Innovation: From Modest Witnessing to Pipeline Thinking*. Basingstoke and New York: Palgrave Macmillan.

Styhre, A. (2013). *A Social Theory of Innovation*. Copenhagen: Copenhagen Business School Press.

Sveiby, K.E. (2007). Disabling the context for knowledge work: The role of managers' behaviours. *Management Decision*, 45(10), 1636–55.

Trice, H.M., and Beyer, J.M. (1993). *The Cultures of Work Organizations*. Englewood Cliffs, NJ: Prentice-Hall.

Vallas, S.P. (2003). The adventures of managerial hegemony: Teamwork, ideology, and worker resistance. *Social Problems*, 50(2), 204–25.

Van Maanen, J. (1991). The smile factory: Work at Disneyland. In P.J. Frost, L.F. Moore, M.R. Louis, C.C. Lundberg, and J. Martin (eds), *Reframing Organizational Culture*. Newbury Park, CA: Sage.

Van Maanen, J. (1995a). Fear and loathing in organization studies. *Organization Science*, 6(6), 687–92.

Van Maanen, J. (1995b). Styles as theory. *Organization Science*, 6(1), 133–43.
Weick, K.E. (1969/79). *The Social Psychology of Organizing*. Reading, MA: Addison-Wesley.

Chapter 2

Accretion, Angst and Antidote: The Transition from Knowledge Worker to Manager in the UK Heritage Sector in an Era of Austerity

ALISTAIR BOWDEN and MALGORZATA CIESIELSKA

The transition from worker to manager requires "a profound psychological adjustment – a transformation of professional identity" (Hill, 2004: 121). The transition from knowledge worker to manager of knowledge workers is particularly difficult. Some professionals find it "a big transition" or "a quantum leap" (Corlett, 2009: 150), whilst others "simply cannot adjust to a managerial life style" (Raelin, 1991: 186). This chapter presents vignettes from a small sample of interviews of a group of knowledge workers – heritage managers in the UK – on their career progressions during turbulent times following the global financial crisis of 2007–2008. These heritage managers began working together as advisors to a community-led heritage organization, though their day jobs and earlier careers were in separate organizations. Each of them was interviewed twice: the first time to gain their individual perspectives on the formation of the community-led heritage organization that they were contributing to; and the second time to explore their own career progression and how it had led them to work together. The semi-structured interviews took place in 2013 and were part of a longitudinal case study.

Based on our findings, we argue that the idea of accretion may be more useful than career progression in this context, and that knowledge workers need greatest support when they cross the chasm to line manage other knowledge workers from multiple professional backgrounds. We also find that public sector managers are having to cope with the repercussions of the global financial crisis, in the form of the austerity policies of the 2010 Conservative–Liberal Democrat coalition government. They feel a sense of angst about the negative preoccupation with repeated cycles of cost saving, staff loss and service reductions within their own organizations. However, perhaps ironically, they find an antidote in contributing to external partnerships that are emerging, at least in part, due to associated austerity policies promoting community leadership. This chapter first introduces the long-term and recent context and the case study in which the heritage managers are involved. It then introduces the heritage managers and explores their career progression, including the point where they work together in the case study organization. Finally it briefly discusses their experiences in relation to the literature on career progression and summarizes the organizational and personal consequences.

Context

The broad context for the case is a long-term trend of the third sector taking on ever greater responsibility for public service delivery in the UK (Macmillan, 2010). This began in the 1990s under a Conservative government where a "contract culture" saw the third sector as alternative providers to the state. It expanded rapidly under the New Labour government of 1997–2010, where a "partnership culture" saw the third sector as partners in the delivery of a large range and ever increasing volume of public service delivery that aspired to create synergy, transformation and/or budget enlargement (Powell and Dowling, 2006). Most recently the Conservative–Liberal Democrat coalition government since 2010 has placed great emphasis on the Big Society, which not only continues the policy of devolving public service delivery to the third sector but also empowers communities, not the state or the professionals it employs, to become the leaders, decision makers and policy setters (Alcock, 2010).

The recent context for the case is the ongoing repercussions of the global financial crisis of 2007–2008 and the era of austerity in the public sector that has resulted. In the UK this began in 2010 when the newly elected coalition government began a programme of major cuts to public sector spending (Taylor-Gooby, 2012). The hardest hit area of the public sector has been local government (LGA, 2013b), and the hardest hit areas of local government are all non-statutory services that are not legally required to be provided (LGA, 2013a). Within this context, museums and heritage are more generally "easy targets" (Newman and Tourle, 2013).

This case study focuses on a heritage-based, third sector organization – the Flodden 1513 Ecomuseum located in the North East of England.[1] When the initial group of community leaders met five years ago, their sole point of focus was to do something to commemorate an anniversary of a significant historical event – the Battle of Flodden. Three things quickly emerged: firstly, many local community groups were already planning a wide range of events to mark the anniversary; secondly, though there was one place that acted as a focal point for the historical event, the full story actually involved many places and some mechanism was needed to include them all; thirdly, to successfully apply for grant funding to commemorate the anniversary, the organizers would have to think about legacy beyond the anniversary itself. In response, an ecomuseum was set up. Rather than a traditional museum – a building, filled with objects, interpreted by specialist curators, to which the public are admitted – an ecomuseum is a community-led "museum without walls" that cares for and makes accessible a place: including the landscape, buildings, objects, wildlife, traditions and myths (Davis, 2011). The organization is now a community enterprise, formally not-for-profit limited company that has successfully won three successively larger grants of £35,000, £85,000 and £875,000. At the core of the ecomuseum is a network of 41 sites and a website that creates a public interface. Grant-funded projects have delivered community archaeology (excavations, metal detecting, field walking) and community documentary research (transcriptions of medieval documents), both aimed at learning more about the historical event, as well as an extensive schools learning programme. There has also been an intense media campaign to raise the profile of the historic event and the ecomuseum as a sustainable economic development tool to attract visitors to the area.

Heritage Managers and their Careers

Four heritage managers were invited by the community leaders to take part in this ecomuseum endeavour. Their role was not to take over and lead, or to provide the funding, but to advise on the general development path – fundraising, project management – and to contribute specialist professional knowledge. They are all mid-career middle managers, but they work for different organizations: three of them work for two different unitary local authorities, whilst the fourth works for a third sector organization that delivers museum, archive and other cultural services.[2]

---

1   See http://www.flodden1513.com
2   It delivers services that were until recently delivered directly by one of the local authorities.

The careers of these different knowledge workers share a common trajectory with similar steps. The following sections use quotes from the interviewees to explore some of the dimensions of their changing roles.

CAREER FOUNDATIONS: KNOWLEDGE WORKERS

Though all four of these managers have responsibility for heritage professionals and service delivery, they have quite different professional roots. All of them started as knowledge workers (Horibe, 1999; Amar, 2002) but in various areas: two of them as heritage professionals, one as a museum curator and the other as an archaeologist. The third began as a marketing professional and the fourth as a sport professional. Their early careers were built on very solid, hard-won foundations. All four have a first degree in their specialism, and one also has a PhD. Three out of the four were also members of their respective professional bodies at the start of their careers, though this was not a requirement for any of them.

Gaining initial full-time professional employment was also difficult and usually required experience that had to be gained by volunteer work or short-term temporary contracts. The museum curator had to take a temporary post, involving moving house with the costs associated. After this ended there was a hiatus with no further positions available. The archaeologist began by running their own business, working as a self-employed draftsman and surveyor for larger, more established fieldwork contractors on large projects. The marketing professional began with a six-month contract, followed by temporary maternity cover. Finally, the sport professional began with a one-year fixed-term contract.

In summary, entry into their chosen fields of knowledge worker involved overcoming significant barriers. However, all four heritage managers had positive memories of their early professional careers. One interviewee had started their career as a curator and spoke of their first museum, which they were in charge of setting up, with distinct pride as "a superb little museum". The marketing professional said:

> *I can remember starting at my first job, I was the most junior member of staff, where I did everything on a project – answering the phone, doing the press releases; it was absolutely brilliant.*

So whilst entry into their professions was hard, the early jobs were universally found to be enjoyable.

EARLY MANAGEMENT RESPONSIBILITIES

All interviewees considered that they began managing very early in their careers, during their first jobs. This was in part due to professional isolation requiring professional advice and some decisions to be made unsupported; for example one interviewee said:

> *Effectively I was the only person working in museums, though I had a line manager who had no museums experience, so it was basically "get on with it" and that has largely been my experience.*

It was also the result of the nature of the professional work which, whilst being knowledge based, essentially involved a significant amount of management tasks. As an example of this, the self-employed archaeologist started to win larger contracts that required significant project management of tasks, budgets and deadlines; but the other three interviewees also had what might be generalized as project management responsibilities.

LEADING KNOWLEDGE WORKERS

The point at which these four heritage managers began line managing staff varied hugely, from six months to over 10 years, and universally they all began by line managing people from their own professions. This first step in managing knowledge workers was relatively seamless. Whilst all interviewees where aware of when it happened, and some reflected self-critically on this moment, they all took it in their stride. With the benefit of hindsight they do not appear to think that this was a major step. However, the more significant step on the career ladder came when they began leading staff from different professional backgrounds, as one interviewee put it: "I do recognize that as a specific point in time". This happened consistently later, between almost 10 years and almost 20 years after the start of their careers.

For three out of four of the heritage managers, there was a self-conscious move to leave their own profession behind and learn about the new profession that they are responsible for. The curator said:

> *I have taken a step back. What I've tried to do is improve my professional knowledge of the other disciplines, so I would concentrate on going to their professional gatherings.*

These three interviewees also started to perceive themselves more as generalists at this time. The marketing professional stated that:

> *... they didn't want anyone who knew anything about running a museum or Anglo-Saxon Britain; they wanted someone who could run a charity, with all the fundraising, marketing, personnel, financial management type stuff, and to be a figurehead.*

Meanwhile the sport professional came to realize that:

> *I can't cram 25–30 years of knowledge and academic study that these guys have got into two to three years because it's in my job description. ... It's not about knowing everything; it's doing the right thing.*

These three heritage managers were also keen to take on the challenge of general management; in the words of one of them: "I was ready for it. I was very, very pleased to get that job". This was in part a sense of repulsion – for example one interview said that "I felt I'd taken museums as far as I could"; but more significantly it was a sense of attraction towards a new challenge. So from a pragmatic point of view it was simply the opportunity to take decisions and build the strategy, and this "being involved at a much higher level" was enjoyable. So, in summary, three out of the four interviewees were positive about this move completely away from their own professional backgrounds and towards managing people from diverse professional backgrounds.

The story of the fourth interviewee, the person who started as an archaeologist, is quite different. Whilst this person has taken on a general management role and now manages people from a number of different professional backgrounds, in their own words they "resent" this transition. The reason this person made the move is in part because they felt that "somebody has to"; but it is also pragmatic "because I wanted the salary". The particular situation has not helped, where they took on the role:

> *We were told it was 25 per cent management and 25 per cent professional work. That has slipped and completely reversed, until around 2008–2009. Now that 25 per cent is getting smaller and smaller – I probably do around 5–10 per cent professional archaeology for the local authority.*

Behind this is a deep professional attachment, where the person would like to be able to be paid their current salary for being a professional archaeologist and they are dancing around this boundary. Two points illustrate this. The first is around their job title, where they are proud of being called County Archaeologist and, though "several bosses have tried to take it off me ... I've subtly fought back". The second is dress code: this person dresses for formal office work as a team manager dressed like a field archaeologist ready to jump into a hole and start excavating at any moment, as another interviewee quite openly said, as his dress code is widely known, "I think everybody knows he's an archaeologist!" This reluctance by no means suggests that this person did not devote themselves consciously and "professionally" to the task of this new general management role. In their own words:

> *It was a learning curve, but not hard – just something that had to be done. I enjoy it, I learn a lot from my fellow professionals and we try to get them to learn from each other, which is always interesting.*

So, in summary, this fourth person is quite different: whilst they have taken on the role of being a general manager and appear to have devoted themselves to the task, they are overtly reluctant to leave behind their professional roots.

LEADING THE COMMUNITY

For the three local authority heritage managers, the necessity of leading communities began when the New Labour government was strongly encouraging the use of partnerships as a means of delivery across the public sector. So it was less of a voluntary step up the career ladder and more of an extra rung that was added to the ladder that had to be stepped up. For the person who has worked in the third sector, it has been a consistent part of their normal day-to-day working. For the curator, this was actually:

> *... the highlight of my career – the period when I started to take a leading role in a [major community regeneration project]. We put together a funding package of about £6 million and it took over five years to the opening of the final phase in 2009. ... As we developed that project we formed a community consultation group and we met once a month, of an evening, for two years as [we] developed the project and they became key stakeholders.*

And in terms of how this way of working is now embedded:

> *Community consultation is built into so much of what we do and what we are expected to do. Also in terms of funding it has to have community support. It's far better if it's community driven.*

The archaeologist shares the positive experience of working with communities: "engaging local communities makes for richer projects", though he is also pragmatic about the necessity to work in partnership with communities when applying to external grant-giving bodies: "Of course I'm a funding whore and the community is key!" In practical terms most engagement with community groups are short, like mini-consultancy assignments often associated with fundraising. However, some community engagement was longer term and in-depth: one project running for a number of years and involving "delivery of training, excavation site direction, producing talk programmes and part way through taking over the management of the entire project".

KNOWLEDGE WORKERS STILL

Following similar steps up the management career ladder, this section reflects on how each heritage manager feels about their original profession. Though it varied, it was quite surprising to find that all four still felt a clear sense that they were still professionals. The most obvious example is the archaeologist, who said that he "would go crazy without some professional time". The curator remains a reviewer for new entrants into the professional body, and still attends the professional conference. The sport professional remains a member of his professional body, and clearly still identifies himself with this profession – though now it is "just one tiny aspect" of his role. Finally, what the marketing professional said is interesting: "I always feel like I'm a practitioner ... [though] if you were to ask me, I'd say I was a Museum Director [but] I've never felt that I've got to that stage where I can just tell other people what to do and not do it myself". More interesting still, when comparing themselves with other managers in the museum and heritage sector, they said: "Sometimes I regret not having a specialism ... sometimes I wish I had been the archaeologist who made it to be Director, as there's more of an interesting story in that".

So all four heritage managers remained aware of their roots and felt some legitimacy, however small, from this core knowledge and expertise. Perhaps most interesting was the view of the person who didn't consider that they had a specialism; but perhaps this is a perspective that has emerged when working in a world where professionals with strong, specialist academic backgrounds in biology, geology, archaeology and history are the norm.

Managing in an Era of Austerity

This final section explores the impact of the 2010 coalition government's policy of austerity that has had a significant impact in terms of budget cuts. Again the impact of these changes differs: the manager in the third sector is least affected, whilst these cuts completely dominate the discourse of the three local authority managers. As an example of the depth of feeling, this quote encapsulates the pressure:

> *Since the bankers fucked the country and the economic crisis has given Labour and the Conservative governments an excuse to give public services a kicking … the need to find savings now is becoming more and more intense. … So that's the focus of my work now, transformation and restructuring [which is a euphemism for making budget cuts, then dealing with the service delivery and organizational consequences].*

Or, as another interviewee described their day job, "Over the past five years it's been a creeping death. More recently it's been cuts on cuts".

The intense negative feelings of the three local authority managers towards their current roles were palpable during the interviews. One alluded to looking for other jobs; another said "There are days when I'd like to stay in bed"; and the other, who is facing dismantling what they have spent many years creating, said with typical understatement, "It's not what I wanted to do in the last few years of my career!" But beyond this codified sense of angst, their non-verbal communication was telling: their body language was limp, slumped; their speech was slow and considered; they looked tired, worn down and resigned.

These three heritage managers therefore find themselves with less fluid budgets and fewer staff. They are now "not doers, but facilitators: enabling, linking people together, not delivering services". Another interviewee said: "Now we're not the cultural leaders, we enable people [in the community] to lead".

So within this context, it might be expected that these four heritage managers may resent their advisory role in the community-led organization to which they all contribute and where they work together – Flodden 1513 Ecomuseum. In many respects it seems to exemplify the way these managers now spend their time, advising and influencing external community-led projects. Yet they unanimously enjoy their input to the ecomuseum. This is represented by comments such as "I do feel very personally attached to Flodden", "of all the projects last year, I probably felt closest to Flodden", "one of the more enjoyable parts of my job", "bright spots in a dark week" and "it's quite refreshing". What lies beneath this enjoyment of the ecomuseum work is in part the contrast with other work, nicely encapsulated by the following quote:

> *It's a positive project, it's going forward, it's achieving something, it's establishing a legacy, it's going forward rather than making cuts.*

But their enjoyment of the ecomuseum work also reflects the positive impact this community-led project is having; for example:

> *[Originally] I was round the table at Flodden because of the potential in terms of profile for the county, how it would contribute to the visitor offer. Whereas I've seen what else it's produced: the sense of pride and how people have got behind it.*

As when talking about their internal roles, their non-verbal communication when talking about Flodden was revealing: they leaned forward, spoke faster, smiled more, were more animated. It is this body language, contrasted with their body language when talking about their day-to-day roles, that is the lingering memory of the second set of interviews.

The particular ways in which the four heritage managers contribute to the Flodden 1513 Ecomuseum varies. All four interviewees assessed their input as overwhelmingly relating to their management expertise, not their professional expertise. In particular, interviewees thought they contributed their knowledge and experience relating to fundraising and project management. Whilst the interviewees clearly felt their input was mainly managerial, participant observations of Steering Group meetings suggest they are consulted and give opinions on areas of professional expertise for which they are responsible (e.g. museums, archives, education, marketing and tourism). So whilst they may feel their own skills in areas such as fundraising are strategically more important and they are conscious that when serious work is required in any professional area (e.g. contributing specialist planning to a fundraising application) they delegate this to subordinate professionals, they do appear to play an important day-to-day professional advisory role in the ecomuseum. Two of the local authority managers also saw their role as acting as a link and conduit of information between the ecomuseum and their respective local authorities, which are key partner organizations. Interestingly, they both saw this as significant and similarly emphasized a translation role, for example "quietly advising the ecomuseum on the best way to deal with the council [and] coming along to meetings and giving a view from the council". Two of the interviewees also felt they played what in their terms was a "leadership" role, not as a chairperson or figurehead but in helping to "drive the vision" and providing a "pragmatic approach to getting things done".

Discussion

Much of the literature on the transition from knowledge worker to manager of knowledge workers assumes this to be a linear process, from junior to senior roles, leaving behind the identity of the previous role at each successive progression. For example, as quoted at the start of this chapter, Hill described this transition as requiring "a profound psychological adjustment – a transformation of professional identity" (2004: 121). However, this study found that the idea of accretion may be more useful than progression: more like the formation of a pearl, with successive layers building up around the kernel of grit in the centre. The professional knowledge that was the foundation of the career continues, albeit in an ever smaller way, to form the kernel of the personal identity of the senior manager.

When the four heritage managers who are involved in the Flodden 1513 Ecomuseum made the transition from knowledge workers to managers of knowledge workers, they do not seem to have experienced the "big transition" or "quantum leap" (Corlett, 2009: 150) described in other studies. However, when they made the further transition to become managers of knowledge workers from multiple professional backgrounds, they all recognized this as a big transition or quantum leap. All four of the managers saw this as a "natural progression" (Raelin, 1991), with three of them simply "moving up" the hierarchy within their professional fields, and only one – the person whose career began as a marketing professional – seeing themselves as a "career manager" (Watson and Harris, 1999).

Yet for the senior heritage managers interviewed in this case study, their early professional careers were a matter of pride, a basis of legitimacy when managing related professionals and advising more senior staff, and finally a touchstone in the current difficult times. A more cumbersome but more accurate and resonant metaphor in this context for their accreted identities might be a priceless object, in a bespoke mount, in a secure display case, within a museum. At the centre is the priceless object (the professional career), around which are the artefacts that show it off, make sense of it, keep it secure and make it accessible.

The angst felt by the three local authority managers is mirrored elsewhere. A survey reported by the Institute of Leadership and Management suggests that 70 per cent of public sector staff feel that "morale is at an all-time low and 43 per cent want to leave their current employer". The problem is "most acute among senior managers, where 84 per cent say morale is at a record low [and] almost one in three (32 per cent) want to quit their job" (Martindale, 2013). The counterbalancing antidote of working with expanding community-led partnerships like the Flodden 1513 Ecomuseum does not appear to have been reported in the trade press or academic literature yet. It is possible that the situation and nature of the ecomuseum is unique and that this phenomenon is not seen elsewhere; or it may be that the satisfaction gained from an advisory role with community-led organizations is an emerging phenomenon that is yet to be reported more widely.

Organizational and Personal Consequences

According to the vignettes in this study, the main transition in the process of career accretion is not the point at which knowledge workers take on management responsibility for delivering activities, husbanding resources and hitting deadlines. Nor is it the point where knowledge workers start line managing knowledge workers, as this initial staff leadership transition feels safe. The main organizational consequence of this research is that knowledge workers need greatest support when they cross the chasm to line manage knowledge workers from multiple professional backgrounds. Formal training and development systems need to be focused at supporting this most difficult and ambiguous transition; and informal line management coaching by knowledge workers who have already made the transition would be valuable.

The main personal consequence for the individuals concerned, which was quite striking when carrying out the interviews, was the deep discontentment felt by the three public sector employees in the current situation. Whilst they feel angst that their internal facing jobs are a negative cycle of austerity cuts and trying to optimistically manage decline, they can find and antidote in their external relationships, like their involvement in the Flodden 1513 Ecomuseum; and responding positively to community-led initiatives (and even trying to act as the catalyst to new initiatives) may be the best route to job satisfaction.

References

Alcock, P. (2010). Building the big society: A new policy environment of the third sector in England. *Voluntary Sector Review*, 1(3), 379–89.

Amar, A.D. (2002). *Managing Knowledge Workers: Unleashing Innovation and Productivity*. Westport, CT: Quorum.

Corlett, S.D. (2009). *Professionals Becoming Managers: Personal Predicaments, Vulnerability and Identity Work*. PhD thesis. University of Northumbria. Available at: http://nrl.northumbria.ac.uk/2690/ (accessed 20 November 2013).

Davis, P. (2011). *Ecomuseums: A Sense of Place*. 2nd edn. London: Continuum.

Hill, L.A. (2004). New manager development for the 21st century. *Academy of Management Executive*, 18(3), 121–6.

Horibe, F. (1999). *Managing Knowledge Workers: New Skills and Attitudes to Unlock the Intellectual Capital in Your Organization*. Toronto and New York: Wiley.

LGA (2013a). *Government Cuts Risk "Failing Communities"*. Local Government Association media release. Available at: http://www.local.gov.uk/media-releases/-/journal_content/56/10180/3984939/NEWS (accessed 20 November 2013).

LGA (2013b). *Spending Round 2013: 26 June 2013*. Local Government Association on-the-day briefing. Available at: http://www.local.gov.uk/c/document_library/get_file?uuid=d3040857-38f6-48eb-a8e8-ba16b7e8414e&groupId=10180 (accessed 20 November 2013).

Macmillan, R. (2010). *The Third Sector Delivering Public Services: An Evidence Review*. Third Sector Research Centre, Working Paper 20. University of Birmingham. Available at: http://epapers.bham.ac.uk/799/ (accessed 20 November 2013).

Martindale, N. (2013). *Does the Public Sector Have a Morale Crisis?* Institute of Leadership and Management. Available at: https://www.i-l-m.com/Insight/Inspire/2013/August/public-sector-morale (accessed 9 December 2013).

Newman, K. and Tourle, P. (2012). Coalition cuts 2: Museums. *History Workshop Journal*, 73, 296–301.

Powell, M. and Dowling, B. (2006). New Labour's partnerships: Comparing conceptual models with existing forms. *Social Policy and Society*, 5(2), 305–14.

Raelin, J.A. (1991). *The Clash of Cultures: Managers Managing Professionals*. Boston, MA: Harvard Business School Press.

Taylor-Gooby, P. (2012). Root and branch restructuring to achieve major cuts: The social policy programme of the 2010 UK coalition government. *Social Policy and Administration*, 46(1), 61–82.

Watson, T.J. and Harris, P. (1999). *The Emergent Manager*. London: Sage.

Chapter 3

Nepotism and Turnover Intentions amongst Knowledge Workers in Saudi Arabia

MARYAM ALHAMADI ALDOSSARI and DOROTA JOANNA BOURNE

In today's global economy, knowledge workers are becoming the engines of growth and the key factor in economic development in the global market (Amar, 2002). Economically developed countries have been investing resources to enrich their human capacity to enhance their competitive position internationally (Shin et al., 2012). Countries in East Asia, for example like China and Japan, are efficiently recognized for employing knowledge-based strategies (Shin and Harman, 2009). In the last few decades Gulf countries, including Saudi Arabia, have started heavily investing financial resources to build their human capital in an attempt to shift their economy from depending solely on oil to a knowledge-based economy (Onsman, 2010). Like many other countries in the region, Saudi Arabia responded to the global trend and started to invest heavily in sending employees overseas in order to compete in the global market and meet the demands of the Saudi employment market (MEP, 2010).

Organizations in Saudi Arabia started sending employees overseas to develop their skills, as employees with international management expertise are now considered to be a competitive resource for any organization (Carpenter et al., 2001). For that reason, international assignments have become an essential part of employees' careers, and for organizations it is a way of attracting, developing and retaining skilled workforce. Nevertheless, studies suggest that an international assignment can be a "double-edged sword" for staff as well as companies. Problems described in the repatriation literature include repatriates' adjustment difficulties, underperformance upon return, and difficulties in retaining these skilled employees, which all generate high costs and are considered to reflect unsuccessful repatriation (Stahl et al., 2009). Although, organizations clearly do not wish to lose valued employees, our primary data shows that the turnover percentage among repatriates is around 40 per cent. The costs to organizations of losing repatriates are massive, both financially and strategically. Typically, a US firm spends in excess of $1 million to send an employee abroad, provide support, and return them home (Black et al., 1999).

This chapter discusses how international assignment was used as a tool to expand knowledge within an organization, using the example of the Kingdom of Saudi Arabia. We focus particularly on the case of repatriation and problems with subsequent staff turnover among repatriates in Saudi Arabia's private sector. Before doing so, the chapter provides a background to the Saudi labour market and the impact of Saudization policies that aimed to reduce reliance on foreign labour. Following this, the chapter discusses the Saudi government's attempt to create a national knowledgeable labour force through international assignment. Finally, using the example of an organization in Saudi Arabia, this chapter illustrates the possible role of Wasta – a prevalent form of nepotism that permeates organizational life in Saudi Arabia – in repatriate managers' turnover intentions. Our focus is on unravelling the impact of Wasta on human resource management (HRM) practices, with a particular focus on the management of the repatriation process of Saudi employees upon their completion of international assignments.

The Saudi Labour Market

The Saudi Arabian labour market presents very distinctive characteristics. It relies largely on foreign workers: only 10 to 15 per cent of employees in the private sector are Saudi nationals, and about 80 per cent of the labour force is non-national (UNDP, 2010). In a country of 19 million people, approximately 7 million are foreigners, representing no less than 60 per cent of the working population and more than 93 per cent of private sector employees (Cooper, 1996). The significant share of foreign employees in the Saudi labour market is a result of high economic growth in Saudi Arabia during the oil boom of the 1970s and early 1980s. This resulted in a shortage of workers who were needed to support the growing economy (Mellahi and Al-Hinai, 2000). This sudden economic boom in Saudi Arabia had an effect on the structure of society at all levels. The government implemented a very extensive development plan, which involved investing in hospitals, housing projects, transportation, universities, schools, airports and other development schemes (Mellahi, 2000). The swift transformation of the economy from an economy based on nomadic trade, fishing and agriculture to an economy based on the hydrocarbon, construction and service industries using modern technological production processes created a need for a new base of skilled workers who were not available locally (Atiyyah, 1996). As a consequence, Saudi Arabia witnessed an enormous influx of foreign employees (Mellahi and Wood, 2002).

Reliance on foreign labour has created unemployment in Saudi Arabia (Prokop, 2003). Unemployment among nationals caused a crisis that has forced the government to take action. Several policies and plans have been implemented by the Saudi government to control the recruitment of those expatriates in the public and private sectors (Looney, 2004). One of the plans which was imposed as a strategic objective by the government to reduce the reliance on expatriates was a Saudization (localization) programme (Madhi and Barrientos, 2003). The aim of Saudization is to replace the expatriate labour force with a trained and qualified local labour force in a planned manner that will support the development of local manpower to create a pool of human resources able to cater for the needs of the economy (Kamal and Al-Harbi, 1997; Mellahi and Al-Hinai, 2000). Overall, the programme has three main goals, which are as follows (Looney, 2004):

- increased employment for Saudi nationals across all sectors of the domestic economy;

- reduced and reversed over-reliance on foreign workers;

- recapture and reinvestment of income which otherwise would have flowed overseas as remittances to foreign worker home countries.

Saudization is a goal that has been hard to accomplish, as new Saudi graduates entering the job market failed to meet the required quality and specializations needed by the labour market (Wapler, 2001). This is due to the present Saudi education system often leaving students lacking in the skills required in the modern business world (Bhuian and Al-Jabri, 1996; Bhuian et al., 2001). The growing mismatch between the educational and technical qualifications of the new entrants and the skill requirements of the market caused a high rate of unemployment among the new graduates. Studies by the International Labour Organization (ILO) and the World Bank have revealed the deficiency of the Saudi education system in effectively preparing Saudis for future jobs, and its gradual negative effect on economic development (Bourland, 2002).

The Saudi government is therefore taking some steps, such as sending Saudi students abroad to obtain education and training, to increase and ensure employment chances for Saudi graduates (MEP, 2010). Saudi Arabia has embraced education and training as the main mechanism for closing the skills gap and career development to create a national knowledgeable labour force (Madhi and Barrientos, 2003). Attempts to reform have been carried out by King Abdullah. The King Abdullah Scholarship Programme has sent 109,000 high-achieving Saudis to pursue graduate studies abroad, mainly in the United States, Europe and the Middle East. These attempts have been made to fill the gap in the education system with a scheme to educate Saudi Arabia's brightest students at foreign universities (MOHE, 2014).

International Assignment and the Repatriation Process

The most commonly practised method of gaining knowledge is an international assignment (Stroh et al., 2000). International assignment gives employees an opportunity to acquire comprehensive knowledge about the national market, culture and the business climate in different countries where their organization operates (Berthoin Antal et al., 2001). Research illustrates that expatriation presents an opportunity to obtain knowledge from international assignments; repatriation presents the opportunity to transfer this knowledge and utilize it within the organization (Black and Gregersen, 1991; Black et al., 1992). However, the possibility of organizational learning exists only if the knowledge acquired by individuals on international assignments can be circulated across the organization.

International assignment represents an opportunity to learn; however, "repatriation failure" raises questions about the waste of such an opportunity. The high rate of repatriation failure, which had been demonstrated by much research (Vidal et al., 2007; Lee and Liu, 2007; Stahl et al., 2009), casts doubt on the role of international assignment towards organizational learning. Extensive research has been done on the repatriate adjustment process (Black and Mendenhall, 1991; Andreason and Kinneer, 2005; Hyder and Lövblad, 2007), repatriation job satisfaction (Vidal et al., 2007, 2008) and turnover intention after repatriation (Stahl et al., 2009; Stroh et al., 2000). Interestingly, there appears to be no empirical research which has focused on the influence of wider cultural attributes shaping organization practices and repatriation processes. The following case study presents Wasta's impact on employees' turnover intention after repatriation from international assignment.

Case Study

Saudi-Co's[1] headquarters are in Dhahran, Saudi Arabia, and subsidiaries are located throughout the Kingdom and around the world: in China, Japan, India, the Netherlands, the Republic of Korea, Singapore, the United Arab Emirates, the UK and the US. For 47 years Saudi-Co was US owned, but the Saudi Arabian government took full control in 1980. After Saudi-Co's transition from a privately held consortium to a pivotal national monopoly, it was important that Saudization was implemented within the organization, and King Abdullah encouraged the senior management in Saudi-Co to take an active role in the internationalization of its workforce so that it could rely less on foreign workers. As a result, today 87 per cent of Saudi-Co employees are Saudi, with 99 per cent of managers being Saudi nationals. Saudi-Co had contributed to the implementation of Saudization by recruiting and training locals.

Throughout Saudi-Co's history there has been an emphasis on developing world-class learning programmes to equip employees with knowledge and skills. Today, the company makes massive investments in training and development – in excess of $10,000 per employee annually and extending across employees' careers. An emphasis is placed on sponsoring employees to pursue university degrees at leading Saudi universities and top-tier education institutions in the US, Europe, China, the Far East and Australia. Out-of-company assignments are another key tool used to develop leadership and technical skills in the company. The company collaborates with its alliance partners throughout the world to place Saudi employees in their firms, exposing them to global practices and diverse technologies. In addition the company also relies on around 12 per cent of its workforce who are non-Saudi professionals from around the world to assist in knowledge transfer around new technologies and management practices.

Saudi-Co's CEO has paid considerable attention to strategically promoting the professional development, skills and knowledge of its national workforce so that it becomes less reliant on migrant workers. Formal organizational policy has been placed in action to ensure that sufficient numbers of employees could be persuaded to take on international assignments in line with the Saudization policy. The organization allocates $1 billion per year to employee recruitment, training and development; this includes sponsoring more than 2,000 employees for educational assignments in different universities around the world. The company runs college foundation programmes which provide Saudi

---

1 Company name has been changed to protect confidentiality.

high-school graduates with the skills to help them succeed in international universities. The company also operates a community college that trains thousands of young Saudis in technical skills that they need for employment. Moreover, the company encourages its employees to continue developing professionally by providing different programmes, such as support for college degrees, advanced degree assignments, advanced medical and dental training programmes, medical professional development programmes; specialist dental training, specialist development, management training, professional and technical training, and international company assignments.

Saudi-Co has two types of international assignment: educational assignment and work assignment. Within educational assignments, every year Saudi-Co sends many employees to attend graduate programmes overseas. The organization will pay tuition and all expenses, in addition to the employees' regular salary. HR managers claim that these assignments are designed thoroughly to fill knowledge gaps in their organization. They also believe that while attending graduate school, Saudi employees gain a better understanding of the broad functioning of foreign businesses and societies. In contrast, within work assignments, lasting on average 18 months, trainees are exposed to factual information about how Saudi-Co's business partners operate their businesses. As trainees, their primary mission was to observe closely and, hence, learn about the company's foreign partners. HR managers claim that the work assignments have been thoroughly studied, carefully planned and well structured to meet business gaps and needs.

While this seems to be a very systematic approach to building the organization's human capital, the majority of repatriate employees at Saudi-Co felt a considerable degree of frustration with both the process and outcome of repatriation. On the whole, repatriates were very dissatisfied with the way the organization managed their overseas experience, and particular concerns included: salary, lack of professional development opportunities, unchallenging tasks, inadequate performance recognition, and insufficient training. As a result of what seemed to be inadequate advance planning, it was often difficult to find a suitable job for the repatriates where their knowledge and experience could be utilized. Although overseas assignments placed employees in s specific position abroad, there was usually no provision on their return to a pre-specified position once an international assignment was completed. Repatriates felt that the company did not really know where to place them once they returned. Many of the repatriates had returned to their pre-assignment position, where they did not utilize the skills and the experiences they had acquired overseas.

A very dominant and important theme which emerged when discussing repatriation concerned interviewees' perception of Wasta. In Saudi society, families are considered the backbone and centre of society (Barakat, 1993). Traditional Saudi Arabian values mandate mutual solidarity and support among extended family members (Abdalla and Al-Homoud, 2001). Therefore, self is defined in relation to family members (Kabasakal and Bodur, 2002) and self-interest is subordinate to the interests of the family. In addition, other in-group relationships, such as friends and tribal members, also have great significance (Rice, 2004). These values therefore promote Wasta where individuals should fulfil what society dictates to be their family and tribal responsibilities (Abdalla et al., 1998). Wasta is one of the main factors of career success. It plays a critical role in hiring and promotion decisions in Saudi Arabia, therefore job security and advancement are generally based on Wasta rather than technical competence or management performance (Rice, 2004). An individual with strong Wasta, even if he/she has poor qualifications, will be favoured over an individual who is more qualified but does not have Wasta (Abdalla et al., 1998; Al-Saggaf and Williamson, 2006). Some authors have suggested that the widespread application of Wasta has resulted in great proportion of the workforce being unqualified and unproductive (Abdalla et al., 1998). Wasta prevents any form of equality by providing undue advantages to groups or individuals who may not necessarily merit them. Metcalfe (2006) has highlighted that training and development opportunities, in addition to managerial recruitment and promotion, largely result from individual relationships and family networks rather than ability.

This was the case in Saudi-Co: repatriates highlighted the way in which the significance of Wasta and its role in career development and progression within the organization was now uppermost in repatriates' minds. Repatriates repeatedly pointed to the fact that *who* you know is more important than *what* you actually know in order to progress in the organization. Wasta was perceived by the majority of the respondents as more important than qualifications and work experience. In order to be promoted you needed to have a family member or friends in high places. When repatriates discussed their lack of career advancement and opportunities upon their return, they emphasized the importance of Wasta over and above qualifications and the skills they had developed on assignment in securing a good job or promotion in Saudi-Co. Wasta was described by repatriates as the magical lubricant that smoothed the way to jobs, promotions, progression in the organization and much else. As a result, repatriates were frustrated to the point where they actually had thought about leaving the company because they felt their experience was not being valued by their managers: 90 per cent of those interviewed stated that they were thinking about leaving their company. Moreover, company documentation highlighted that employees who go on international assignment were about 41 per cent more likely to voluntarily leave Saudi-Co on their return than their peers who did not go on these assignments.

This chapter presents a case study illustrating nepotism or so-called Wasta as a factor strongly contributing to repatriate turnover in Saudi Arabia. The results demonstrate that repatriate employees return from overseas assignments with a wealth of knowledge which they are eager to transfer and apply in their home organization. However, the adaptation of this knowledge is problematic due to the dominance of Wasta that affects an organization's policies and practices.

References

Abdalla, H.F., Maghrabi, A.S. and Raggad, B.G. 1998. Assessing the perceptions of human resource managers toward nepotism: A cross-cultural study. *International Journal of Manpower*, 19, 554–70.

Abdalla, I.A. and Al-Homoud, M.A. 2001. Exploring the implicit leadership theory in the Arabian Gulf States. *Applied Psychology*, 50, 506–31.

Al-Saggaf, Y. and Williamson, K. 2006. Doing ethnography from within a constructivist paradigm to explore virtual communities in Saudi Arabia. *Qualitative Sociology Review*, 2, 5–20.

Amar, A.D. 2002. *Managing Knowledge Workers: Unleashing Innovation and Productivity*. Westport, CT: Quorum.

Andreason, A. and Kinneer, K. 2005. Repatriation adjustment problems and the successful reintegration of expatriates and their families. *Journal of Behavioral and Applied Management*, 6, 109–26.

Atiyyah, H.S. 1996. Expatriate acculturation in Arab Gulf countries. *Journal of Management Development*, 15, 37–47.

Barakat, H. 1993. *The Arab World: Society, Culture, and State*. Berkeley, CA: University of California Press.

Berthoin Antal, A., Lenhardt, U. and Rosenbrock, R. 2001. Barriers to organizational learning: Cases from public health. In M. Dierkes (ed.), *Handbook of Organizational Learning and Knowledge*. Oxford: Oxford University Press, 865–85.

Bhuian, S.N. and Al-Jabri, I.M. 1996. Expatriate turnover tendencies in Saudi Arabia: An empirical examination. *International Journal of Organizational Analysis*, 4, 393–407.

Bhuian, S.N., Al-Shammari, E.S. and Jefri, O.A. 2001. Work-related attitudes and job characteristics of expatriates in Saudi Arabia. *Thunderbird International Business Review*, 43, 21–32.

Black, J.S. and Gregersen, H.B. 1991. Antecedents to cross-cultural adjustment for expatriates in Pacific Rim assignments. *Human Relations*, 44, 497–515.

Black, J.S., Gregersen, H.B. and Mendenhall, M.E. 1992. *Global Assignments: Successfully Expatriating and Repatriating International Managers*. San Francisco, CA: Jossey-Bass.

Black, J.S., Gregersen, H.B., Mendenhall, M.E. and Stroh, L.K. 1999. *Globalizing People Through International Assignments*. Reading, MA: Addison-Wesley.

Black, J.S. and Mendenhall, M.E. 1991. The U-curve adjustment hypothesis revisited: A review and theoretical framework. *Journal of International Business Studies*, 22(2), 225–47.

Bourland, B. 2002. *Saudi Arabia's Employment Profile*. Riyadh: Saudi American Bank.

Carpenter, M.A., Sanders, G. and Gregersen, H.B. 2001. Bundling human capital with organizational context: The impact of international assignment experience on multinational firm performance and CEO pay. *Academy of Management Journal*, 44(3), 493–511.

Cooper, J. 1996. Putting the kingdom to work. *Middle East Economic Digest*, 40, 55–9.

Hyder, A.S. and Lövblad, M. 2007. The repatriation process: A realistic approach. *Career Development International*, 12, 264–81.

Kabasakal, H. and Bodur, M. 2002. Arabic cluster: A bridge between East and West. *Journal of World Business*, 37, 40–54.

Kamal, M. and Al-Harbi, A.S. 1997. Markov analysis of Saudization in engineering companies. *Journal of Management in Engineering*, 13, 87–91.

Lee, H.W. and Liu, C.H. 2007. An examination of factors affecting repatriates' turnover intentions. *International Journal of Manpower*, 28, 122–34.

Looney, R. 2004. Saudization: A useful tool in the kingdom's battle against unemployment? *Journal of South Asian and Middle Eastern Studies*, 27, 13–33.

Madhi, S.T. and Barrientos, A. 2003. Saudisation and employment in Saudi Arabia. *Career Development International*, 8, 70–77.

Mellahi, K. 2000. Human resource development through vocational education in Gulf Cooperation Countries: The case of Saudi Arabia. *Journal of Vocational Education and Training*, 52, 329–44.

Mellahi, K. and Al-Hinai, S.M. 2000. Local workers in Gulf co-operation countries: Assets or liabilities? *Middle Eastern Studies*, 36, 177–90.

Mellahi, K. and Wood, G. 2002. Desperately seeking stability: The making and remaking of the Saudi Arabian petroleum growth regime. *Competition and Change*, 6, 345–62.

MEP, 2010. *The Ninth Development Plan 2010–2014*. Riyadh: Ministry of Economy and Planning.

Metcalfe, B.D. 2006. Exploring cultural dimensions of gender and management in the Middle East. *Thunderbird International Business Review*, 48, 93–107.

MOHE (Saudi Ministry of Higher Education), 2014. *King Abdullah Scholarships Program* [online]. Available at: http://www.mohe.gov.sa/en/default.aspx [accessed 12 May 2014].

Onsman, A. 2010. Dismantling the perceived barriers to the implementation of national higher education accreditation guidelines in the Kingdom of Saudi Arabia. *Journal of Higher Education Policy and Management*, 32, 511–19.

Prokop, M. 2003. Saudi Arabia: The politics of education. *International Affairs*, 79, 77–89.

Rice, G. 2004. Doing business in Saudi Arabia. *Thunderbird International Business Review*, 46, 59–84.

Shin, J.C. and Harman, G. 2009. New challenges for higher education: Global and Asia-Pacific perspectives. *Asia Pacific Education Review*, 10, 1–13.

Shin, J.C., Lee, S.J. and Kim, Y. 2012. Knowledge-based innovation and collaboration: A triple-helix approach in Saudi Arabia. *Scientometrics*, 90, 311–26.

Stahl, G.K., Chua, C.H., Caligiuri, P., Cerdin, J.L. and Taniguchi, M. 2009. Predictors of turnover intentions in learning-driven and demand-driven international assignments: The role of repatriation concerns, satisfaction with company support, and perceived career advancement opportunities. *Human Resource Management*, 48, 89–109.

Stroh, L.K., Gregersen, H.B. and Black, J.S. 2000. Triumphs and tragedies: Expectations and commitments upon repatriation. *International Journal of Human Resource Management*, 11, 681–97.

UNDP, 2010. *The Millennium Development Goals Report*. New York: United Nations Development Programme.

Vidal, M.E.S., Valle, R.S. and Aragón, M.I.B. 2007. Antecedents of repatriates' job satisfaction and its influence on turnover intentions: Evidence from Spanish repatriated managers. *Journal of Business Research*, 60, 1272–81.

Vidal, M.E.S., Valle, R.S. and Aragón, M.I.B. 2008. International workers' satisfaction with the repatriation process. *International Journal of Human Resource Management*, 19, 1683–702.

Wapler, F. 2001. Sponsors in Saudi Arabia: Myths and realities. *Arab Law Quarterly*, 16(4), 366.

Chapter 4

Knowledge Work and the Problem of Implementation: The Case of Engineering

LARS BO HENRIKSEN

Most engineers would nod silently to themselves in quiet sympathy in recognition of the problems Isambard Kingdom Brunel faced when embarking on the project of constructing yet another elegant and functional bridge. The calculations are the easiest part, but human nature ... oh, dear! Whatever the logic, precision and elegance of the calculations, one ignores the human element in implementing such "calculations" at one's peril.

Bjarke and Jesper are engineers in The Company, and they are assigned to different tasks and projects in production management. They both take pride in their identity as engineers and they very willingly relate stories about their work, both their successes and their disappointments. It is, though, evident that their project successes are mostly connected to technologies, and that the project disappointments are much more closely connected to issues related to cooperation with colleagues and other parties – the human element. So what they face is, in many ways, very similar to what the engineers of yesteryear had to deal with; a kind of dual challenge: technology and human nature or technology and culture, technology and the social. Does this then require a dual competence? Do engineers have to live in some kind of schizophrenic state where dealing with technology, as broadly defined, is the right, easy, fun part of engineering; and dealing with colleagues and the social is the cumbersome, unpredictable, messy part that engineers might be better off trying to avoid if at all possible? This is the kernel of what is of concern here: is it the case that engineers are more comfortable when dealing with technology than when dealing with fellow human beings? And do they have to have some kind of dual competence in order to meet the professional challenges that they face in their everyday working lives as engineers? And, if this is the case, what can we do about it? Engineers often call this problem the implementation problem: that is, the technology is thought out, designed and developed; and when that part is over, then comes the tricky part – implementing the technological solution. In this chapter I will analyse this implementation problem with the specific purpose of finding ways of conceptualizing this seemingly dual challenge of engineering which, in most cases, is quite simply unavoidable.

Implementation, literally, means a tool or to fill something into (something); in our everyday conversations 'to implement' means to launch, to realize, to execute, to do it. Referring to Jesper and Bjarke's work, implementation most often means that a known or newly developed technology is to be installed in The Factory. This, however, often proves to be difficult; there is nearly always something that does not go according to the original plan. This is the problem: how do engineers solve the problem they call implementation? In order to investigate this, I conversed with and listened to the stories of Jesper and Bjarke and how they deal with this "implementation" problem. These stories resulted in a new or reinterpretation of the implementation process. In addition to Jesper and Bjarke's stories, we held a workshop where I presented these new interpretations of the implementation process to all other engineers in the department. This workshop added further new perspectives, and samples of both stories and workshop discussions are included here for illustrative purposes.

Engineers

Both Jesper and Bjarke are engineers trained in production management. They both started as trainees in The Company in their final year of studies at engineering school. After graduation they were both employed in The Company and continued the work they had begun during their traineeships. The first task was to work on the PRO1 project – a classic production optimization exercise. Bjarke relates that it was a project concerned with a change of the factories in The Company "from craft to industrial".

Q: How was it before?

Bjarke: Well, it was quite crafts based. It was, it worked the way that we had ... down in some corner they had some regulators, which were produced. And in there, the team leader knew that he had 15 men. But he did not know when there was a regulator that was ready to come out; and he did not really know how efficiently they worked there ...

Q: No.

Bjarke: ... and did not know the requirements for extra resources, so to say. Now if, for example, there is something wrong, or he needs some regulators very fast, then he has to go down to his group and ask, when will a regulator [be ready to come] out? Then they say – that will take the first three hours, or they can say, it will take about five minutes.

Q: Yes.

Bjarke: They can say, eh, well, I need to, we need five more men, or we must work overtime, or we'll be in on Saturday to reach [the goals], or something like that. He cannot control [the process], so he effectively has no power over the line.

Q: No.

Bjarke: The way things are today [after the changes], now it is all managed on stroke-boards, from the morning, based on the number of men, the desired output that you want ... you form the team to man the line.

Q: Yes.

Bjarke: So he can control it. Eh, what can I say, stroke for stroke, whether they can deliver what they are supposed to deliver. At the same time, there is quality – when you know your operations, and they are consistent across departments and factories, so you can better optimize your quality. Before you could – you could not go into such a mess and try to optimize things.

This then was the task: to introduce industrial measures and processes in the production of what Bjarke calls "regulators". Both Bjarke and Jesper note that their jobs, and the work on the PRO1 project, are interesting and challenging. They also tell us that it is somehow different from what they expected on the basis of what they were taught at engineering school. "We do a lot of coordination in this job", notes Jesper. When talking about his work on the PRO1 project, Jesper continues:

There were two engineers in each group ... ehm ... and then there were some blue-collar workers. So we were really like, I do not know if you

> can call it "deputy project managers", but it was certainly a little in that direction, where we, we should, eh, what can I say, on the one hand we had to coordinate the projects a little, that the – the overall project manager – he had set out the plans for what it should look like. But then, on the other hand, we were to execute it and maintain its status; now it is running like that. [Q: Yes] And then fine-tune the schedule in relation to it. So it was very much like maintaining an overview, it was very … and maintain the status, to follow the project plan.
>
> Q: What did you spend most time on?
>
> Jesper: I think it was, it was basically half and half in relation to the coordinating part, the project management part, and then to sit with the thing itself [emphasis by the author], sitting and doing, what should the line look like? Build it up, the workbench must stand there and such and such and so on. So it was approximately half and half; that is my feeling when thinking back on it. It's just about remembering correctly. Ehm, yeah. It's such a little, eh, a little funny to think that when you come from the [engineering] school that you are such, you imagine, that you come out and will do some hard-core engineering work, but much of it is really about coordination instead, at least for the things that I have been involved in.

We note here that Jesper clearly distinguishes between coordination of the implementation process and "the thing itself", what he perceives to be real engineering. To Jesper, being a production engineer is mainly about developing the technology.

> Jesper: And then there is the other side of this, it was, it was what we might call the production engineering part of it. Where we, eh, yes we designed how the lines should look in relation to the demands and wishes that existed. And we, eh, yes, would like to have people just agree that that was how we … the way we do it. Eh, and by listing some pros and cons, use some decision matrices once in a while if it was a somewhat tough decision. And then there was the design of the line. Eh implementing it. And, yes, we worked a lot with standards in relation to it, it was later … with standard cells, eh, standard equipment where we helped to define what type of equipment we wanted, and ehm, then there is the whole process … that you have a need, that we wish to have their standards, and then find what – on a conceptual level – what are

these standards that we want? Well okay, this is it. We'd like to build the entire plant into small squares, then we can move it all around as we wish.

Q: Yes.

Jesper: Just as with small building blocks. That is the conceptual level.

This part of Jesper's story clearly defines engineering as a dual challenge where "the thing itself", real engineering, is contrasted with the coordination, much of it social, that is necessary for implementation. This distinction made by engineers is nothing new and has been discussed by others who have studied the same phenomenon (e.g., Bucciarelli, 1994). Trevelyan (2007, 2009), for example, argues strongly that engineering is both technological and social, and that the social part is every bit as important as the technological – and, as I emphasize here, often more so. Even if Trevelyan (2007) finds that some (many) engineers do not consider the social part "real engineering" and that they dislike "all that administrative stuff", Bjarke and Jesper can only confirm his original findings. The problem now is – what we can do about it? How do we deal with this seemingly split interpretation that prevents engineers from viewing their own work as consisting of *both* technology and the social, because this split interpretation unquestionably creates an amount of misunderstanding, and quite often extreme frustration, of how engineers view their own professional day-to-day working lives, especially when they have to deal with "all that administration" and/or coordination instead of "the thing itself", as Jesper puts it, what engineers perceive to be "real" engineering? How do we transcend this split interpretation? Is it possible to transcend it? Let us explore some more.

Taylor, Post-Fordism and the Implementation Problem

Taylor (1911) was onto the problem. He wanted to create a production system that would result in reduced waste and enhanced productivity for the benefit of all – employer and employee alike. Taylor's means of doing so was "scientific management", or "Taylorism" as it has also become known. Taylor's main idea, the foundation of his production system, was to get rid of waste, hence becoming ever more efficient in producing still more with less. The initial focus of scientific management in achieving this goal was to do away with some of the fallacies of what Taylor called "the old system". The old system can, to some extent, be viewed as equivalent to The Company before the

PRO1 project; that is, craft-based and without much coordination. In the old system the work was organized in independent workshops that functioned as independent sub-suppliers to the factory; in this earlier production system that Taylor detested, the foremen were kings. The foremen hired and fired; they created the work conditions; and they were very often quite nasty and mean. Taylor was obsessive about changing this, so he removed the authority from these foremen. How? He created a uniform set of rules and regulations for the entire factory; the idea was that everybody – workers, foremen and managers – recognized these rules and could trust them. The workers would no longer be handed over to the unpredictable nature and dubious mercies of the foremen. With this change, it became possible to introduce production planning. Prior to this change, coordinated production planning between departments simply did not exist, and Taylor introduced cross-departmental planning, again in order to reduce waste and enhance efficiency. Perhaps the best known of Taylor's ideas were his time and motion studies, stopwatches and centralized determination of accords and payments. This was part of his strategy of freeing these from the tyranny of the foremen's arbitrary whims and determinations. In addition to this, Taylor also introduced more technical measures such as maintenance management and optimization of the use of machines for the sake of energy saving and workload. This all sounds fine – who would not want to reduce waste, and who would not like to work under known, and reasonably fairly determined, work conditions?

But the system still had some severe problems, because one of the main foundations of Taylor's system was the separation of thinking and doing, of planning and execution, of conceptualizing and doing. This separation introduced the implementation problem. That is, managers should think, plan and design the work and the workers should just ... well, work – do it; no more, no less. In this system, separation of technology and the human becomes central; and whatever its original efficiency in its time and place, its resultant problems are now well known in terms of deskilling, cumulative trauma disorder, worker frustration etc. But it seems that the frustration over this separation – the split between human and technology felt by Brunel and by modern engineers – was a constitutive part of Taylor's original system and therefore an unavoidable conflict was built into it, with consequences that resonate right up to the present day. The separation between technology and the human, and its consequent conflicts, were solved in a very brutal manner in Taylor's system: humans were treated as machines, and thereby everything – even the workers in the factory – was turned into technology or somehow conflated with technology; the human becomes the silent, unthinking, submissive cog in the wheel. This solved the problem in the first instance – at least in theory. By eliminating the human factor in the production process Taylor thought that he could eliminate what he called waste. It turned out, of course, that the human factor could not be eliminated so easily then; nor can it be eliminated now short of total automation or robotics. Not even promises of higher pay and/or better incentive schemes could do anything about it. Humans are humans and will remain so even in a Taylorist system.

Moving on from Taylor, the Human Relations school, and later the post-Fordist production methods, reintroduced humans to thinking about production systems. This was definitely also the case for Bjarke and Jesper when they worked on the PRO1 project. The PRO1 project is a child of post-Fordist production methods (Jaffee, 2008: 131) such as Lean, Kanban, Single-Minute Exchange of Die (SMED), etc. One of the features of this system is the involvement, thinking involvement alien to Taylor, of middle managers and blue-collar workers in the production process. The human is being brought back in; again – not that the human ever really left in the first place. People in the factory are no longer simply reduced to, or perceived as, robots in a fixed system, but should themselves understand and master the system and be part of the construction or continuous reconstruction of the system. But, as easily discerned from the stories related by Bjarke and Jesper, the exasperating split between the human and technology remains evident and pervasive – "half and half" says Jesper – and continues to cause serious problems for engineers. The frustration is evident in their conversations, and the engineering school did not provide them with much of a theoretical or practical nature to address or understand, let alone handle or somehow cope pragmatically with this conflict. The distinction between coordination (the human part) and the *real* engineering (the technological part) leads Bjarke and Jesper, and everyone else confronted with post-Fordist production methods, to use the word implementation: that is, engineers are deemed to be calculating, designing and planning the one best production system. This planned system is then implemented in the (social) world of the production system. In this implementation process the fixed plan will inevitably meet resistance and cause conflict.

(Fixed) Plan => Implementation (in fixed setting) => New Factory

In this respect, post-Fordist methods and tools remain grounded in the same basic principles as the original Taylorist ones, if polished up somewhat – a kind of fixed plan that can be implemented; yet the split is still there, as well as the problems inherent in this form of dualistic thinking. How do we transcend this dualism in order to overcome it?

The Critique: The Diffusion Theory

The implementation of a supposedly fixed technology has been intensely critiqued by what has become known as actor network theory (ANT), or science and technology studies (STS) (Latour, 1993; Law and Hassard, 1999; Callon, 1986; Harman, 2009). The critique is here targeted at what is called the diffusion theory or paradigm (Latour, 1987: 133). This is a conception of the development of technological systems – similar to the PRO1 project that Jesper and Bjarke worked on – where the engineer develops the idea of a technological solution. This could be Jesper and Bjarke's production concept that was a piece of paper (or several pieces) describing the intended new industrialized factory. This idea will then somehow travel or diffuse into society (the factory) where it is implemented, or it will be prevented from entering into society, not implemented. In simple terms, it will be a success or a failure. The implementation of the idea is a matter of acceptance; society will either accept the idea or the idea will be rejected. This is what Jesper described above when he talked about coordination and follow-up; implementation took up almost half their time and they could only spend half of the time on *the thing itself*.

There are, however, several problems with this supposed diffusion of technologies. First, the implementation itself. The idea is that the engineer formulates the idea about what the factory should look like (the production concept). This was then implemented into a more or less hostile environment. This is the inertia that slows down the implementation process. People do not necessarily like the idea or they do not understand it. The other part of the diffusion theory is that the original idea will remain more or less the same no matter what kind of resistance it meets. The diffusion theory then explains success and failure in two different ways. If a technology is successful it is because it was a very good idea in the first place and it is only natural that it be accepted and implemented. If it is a failure, on the other hand, it is because of the resistance in the society or social group that is to receive the idea. But this cannot be the case, because success is explained as a natural thing and failure as a social thing; this is illogical. Thereby we can explain anything and, therefore, nothing. We need the same kind of explanation for both success and failure, what Latour (1987: 136) terms the "principle of symmetry".

Yet another, and just as critical, problem is the fact that the diffusion theory presupposes a society or social setting that is predetermined and fixed. Into this fixed social entity the idea is then implemented. Again, this cannot be the case: any new technology introduced into a social entity will eventually change this entity; consequently, it cannot be a fixed entity. Just as the basic idea of the

PRO1 project was to change the factory and the realities of the people working there, if it were fixed it would not be possible. It follows that we need other ways of understanding and explaining this process.

This critique could also be applied to Jesper's (first) description of his job as a production engineer. Half and half, he said: half his job concerns *the thing itself* and the other half concerned coordination or implementation. At first glance, this fits neatly with the diffusion theory. The production engineering concept describes the new factory and what it should look like. This plan and the ideas behind it will meet resistance when introduced to the factory (inertia). It also requires a distinction between the technology (which is fixed) and the social setting (the factory), which is also fixed. This causes problems, as it is difficult to unite two fixed systems without changing either of them. No wonder the process of implementation is perceived as a difficult one from this perspective, sometimes even frustrating. "I spend far too much time on local politics", as one engineer once put it.

The Translation Alternative

Translation is Latour's concept for describing the process of making or creating technological systems (Latour, 1987: 108; Callon, 1986; see also Latour, 1993). A sociology of translation, as proposed by Latour, could look something like this: the central concepts are *actors, actants, networks* and *translation*. For our purposes here, translation is to the forefront in addressing our focal duality or "split". Even if the vast literature on actor network theory (ANT) has explored these concepts meticulously, and in a rather complex fashion, I will settle here for the simpler explanation that actors are human beings and actants are all those manmade things we normally call, devices, technologies etc. Each actor and each actant are granted their status and importance according to their position in the network. This very short description would not go down particularly well with most protagonists of actor network theory, but will be maintained here as it is sufficient for illustrative purposes.[1] Translation, then, refers to describing the process that grants status and importance. The concept was originally borrowed from Serres (Callon, 1986; Brown, 2002) and it is called translation because it is a process of mediation that simultaneously transfers and distorts a signal. In actor network theory this means that actors and actants are granted

---

1 This distinction between actors and actants adopted here is not necessarily in accordance with orthodox actor network theory, but because of the outcomes from the workshop mentioned above this distinction is maintained in this chapter. I shall return to this problem later.

their status in the network through this process; and not as diffusion where the idea travels undistorted through societies, but in a process where each actor/actant receives, interprets and accepts or rejects. This can be described, if again somewhat crudely, as processes of *problematization, interessement, enrolment* and *mobilization of allies* (see Latour, 1987: 108; Callon, 1986: 24–8).

Problematization is the conceptualization of the problem that needs to be solved. It is also about finding the relevant actors, as they need to be identified – who do we need in the project? In Jesper and Bjarke's case the problem was the new factory, as described in the PRO1 project. During problematization, the primary actors – in this case the actors responsible for the PRO1 project – tried to establish themselves as an *obligatory passage point* between the other actors and the network, so that they become indispensable for the project, and for the other actors. This proved to be no easy task – "We did a lot of coordination" – because another aspect of translation is *interessement*, which refers to getting the actors interested and negotiating the terms of their involvement. During the first phases of the PRO1 project the project managers worked hard to convince the other actors that the roles they had defined for them were acceptable. In this particular case they could, drawing on the conventions of the managerial hierarchy, command the other actors to participate, so this was not in question. However, as different modes of participation exist, and in order to make the project work, it was necessary to ensure that all actors accepted their participatory roles in the project and that they would actively try to achieve its goals. Passive resistance and neglect, for example, are well-known modes of resistance. Because of the different interpretations – translations – and because of the insecurities following these different interpretations, and because of misunderstandings following the unclear conceptualizations of project means and goals, the *interessement* process proved to be difficult. The next process is called *enrolment*, where the actors accept the project and the roles that have been defined for them during interessement. Finally, one experiences the *mobilization of allies* stage or phase. When each actor has been granted and accepted a project role, they will need to mobilize allies in their network in order to be able to fulfil that role. In Jesper and Bjarke's case, for example, these could refer to other engineers in other departments; suppliers from other companies; managers higher up in The Company's hierarchy; or anyone else who could be useful and could contribute to the project, and without whom the project might be doomed to fail.

This is not to say that the processes of problematization, interessement, enrolment and mobilization of allies are stages as in a linear stage model, but as processes that are continuously negotiated between the actors (see also

Henriksen et al., 2004: 163). They should, rather, be visualized and understood as ongoing processes that are present, in different forms and with different strengths, throughout the lifetime of the project. Sometimes discourses (conceptualization), social settings (structures) and technologies (actants) are temporarily fixed in the process, and thereby stabilize the process: for example, when the engineers have reached a milestone; conducted a production line to run to the required specifications; or established an agreement with a supplier of factory equipment.

With this description of the project as a translation process we can escape from, or transcend, several of the problems noted above in the diffusion model. The network, the ideas, the discourses, the technologies and the social settings are not fixed; the changes written into the PRO1 project charter are not simply a matter of naively implementing fixed technologies in fixed and hostile environments, but can now be viewed as a much more dynamic process of interpretation, negotiation, conflict resolution and changing alliances. It is a complex process where actors, actants and networks are temporarily fixed and then dissolved again in both stable and volatile arrangements.

The question now is whether this description of the PRO1 project, and Jesper and Bjarke's roles in the process, does more justice to the actual process than the implementation process as described by Jesper and Bjarke above. They both told another story about the project, and the structure of these stories looks far more like a translation process than the diffusion process described in the first story.

Jesper and Bjarke on Translation

Might this method or "translation" lens provide a better description of Bjarke and Jesper's PRO1 project and their work in implementing it? Maybe it would, because by acknowledging the project as a dynamic process that gradually established the kind of production system that the project plan envisaged we gain some deeper insights. It allows us to recognize that this process is social, discursive and real (Latour, 1993) – that the process consists of actors and actants in a network that interacts with and sometime fixes discourses, social relations and technologies, if only temporarily.

When asked about his everyday work, Jesper tells a slightly different story to the story he told when he was asked about what it is like being an engineer:

> So on the detailed level; gosh, what is going to be inside the small squares? It should, it should look like this and it should have these tolerances. And, yes, what kind of equipment do we need? It must be able to do this, so there has been a lot of contact with suppliers, also, in terms of specifications, what kind of equipment do we need? Eh, get it written down in some ...
>
> Q: Machine suppliers?
>
> Jesper: Yes, the machine supplier. It might be workbenches, it could be cranes, it could be different things. Ehm, so it is about getting specifications made to them, engage in dialogue with them, to get ... to find out what exactly it is we want. Because, in the beginning, we do not really quite know. [Q: No.] We know we want a workbench, but we have a lot of products that will hopefully fit into them, how do we get them to fit? [Q: Yes.] So along the way, you will get smarter, better at it. So it's such a ... what can you call it, a collaboration with the suppliers.

Bjarke relates a similar story:

> Q: So it was simply classic production engineering work, designing the line?
>
> Bjarke: Yes. You can say that. So you are in and try to optimize and make suggestions about how such a [line], what it should look like.
>
> Q: Okay.
>
> Bjarke: Ehm, and then you are out there [in the factory] and you ask about ... whether people agree, if we can make it work.

We see here that dialogue and cooperation are essential parts of the project because "we do not know what we want"; therefore, the process of producing the final production system is discursive, social and real. It is discursive in the sense that the engineers do not know what they want; but gradually, through dialogue, they create a language and they conceptualize the concepts that are able to handle and describe the project. This was not fixed in the production concepts or blueprints, but had to be developed. Simultaneously, the engineers had to develop the social relations with the "interested parties", as they call them: suppliers of equipment, colleagues and partners in The Company.

"Interested parties" is a very precise description of the actors involved, because all involved in the process had interests and wanted to contribute to the negotiations that established the production system. They are also real in the sense that the actants also had to be taken seriously in the process. The technology involved, such as the workbenches, also had to be negotiated; and the final layout of the factory is not fixed *ab initio*, as naively presented in the diffusion implementation model discussed above – or in the initial plan that the engineers produced. The technologies, the actants, are changed, modified while also restricting what is possible in the implementation process due to some of their own internal constraints. The technologies definitely have a say in this: "and then you are out there [in the factory] and ask about ... whether people agree, if we can make it work".

With this description of the process the role of the engineer must now be viewed somewhat differently; at a minimum, engineers should try to understand their own role in the implementation process. They are not simply the pure engineers who once and for all calculate and design a fixed plan (the engineering part, "the thing itself") that has to be implemented and then spend their time coordinating this implementation (the project management part). This was what caused the frustration, because the implementation did not work as smoothly as the engineers would have wished – because of the inertia. But how could they? As they noted themselves, they did not know what they wanted; nor were they sure how it would work in the factory. The plan, quite simply, was not fixed; rather, they themselves engaged in a process of translation. They problematized and formulated the problem. They themselves called this making a production concept; that is the plan that sketched out the factory they wished to see materialize sometime in the future. They managed to get their colleagues interested in the project, which was sometimes more difficult than they would have liked. In these processes of interessement and enrolment they attempted to convince the other partners so that they accepted their roles in the project. Finally, they mobilized allies and succeeded in getting them to actively support and work on the project. When asked what they were doing in their everyday lives, both Jesper and Bjarke actually told stories of translation. "We did not know what we wanted", said Jesper; and therefore they engaged in a dialogue with colleagues, suppliers and everyone else who could possibly contribute to the project. In this way, through dialogue, Jesper and Bjarke engaged themselves in a process better described as translation, and thereby they were better able to manage the project. Strange as it now may seem, they still think that this translation process is not the right way to do it; and they also told a story of (failed) implementation and the frustration that this caused. They made a plan and they expected that their job was to implement this plan. They found out that the plan was inadequate for the factory and the type of production system that they wanted, and they found out that they had to do something else. This first plan was not implemented; instead the plan was changed or "opened up" for negotiations and a process of translation could get started – and this process was very successful. When negotiation replaced implementation things started to get going and real progress was made.

Strange, though, that they still think of this process of translation as "not the right way"; and strange that they were frustrated by the failed implementation. This can only be because they expected something else; that they have a certain, perhaps too rigid, idea about their job in their heads – and the job, in reality, turned out to be of a different kind. Once again the split, which continues to beg the question how to transcend it.

The Split, Once Again: The Workshop

This split between technology and the social, between nature and culture, is patently obvious and evident through the experiences of engineers of yesteryear up to modern-day engineers, and within engineering schools and in more recent philosophical debates (e.g. Latour, 1993). All seem to agree that the split exists; and all appear to be somewhat troubled by it. Practitioner engineers exhibit annoyance and frustration at the necessity of coordination and administration, as these tasks are viewed as getting in the way of the real thing. Students of industry and technology find it problematic because the split forces them to describe the technology as social, discursive, or real (Latour, 1993). The key question now is whether the translation alternative discussed above might help engineers, such as Bjarke and Jesper, to better understand their projects and, perhaps more importantly, through transcending this 'split' reach a better and more realist understanding of their own engineering profession. From their training, and probably also from a very strong engineering tradition, they have an image of engineering work as "the thing itself" (Jesper's key phrase), and an image of coordination/administration as somewhat of a distracting nuisance that they would prefer to do without. This split between technology and the social is well known and institutionalized in our schools, colleges and universities. In the curricula at engineering schools this split is very evident. While "the thing itself" is granted a very central place, for very good technical and professional reasons subjects like project management and organization studies are only marginally included in such curricula, if included at all.

Returning to the engineers, how do they handle the split and how do they talk about it? At a workshop conducted during the summer of 2011 I presented the ideas of an implementation process described as a translation process, and using the language of actor network theory (ANT) as briefly noted above. At the workshop 11 of the department's engineers were present; all had a background in production management, even if they specialized in certain aspects of production management and worked on different production-related tasks. At this workshop the ideas were well received and the presentation became the basis for interesting discussions among the engineers. They all clearly recognized the problem; they also recognized the frustration they felt when dealing with this split in engineering projects – administration/coordination and "the thing itself". This dilemma was very well known, experientially, and all were eager to discuss it and, more importantly, try to possibly do something about it. That said, they were also quite critical of the vocabulary of actor network theory and some contested discussions emerged on this within the workshop group.

After my introductory presentation a vibrant discussion emerged on the concept of translation and the concept of actants. First the concept of translation was replaced by "negotiation", as most of the engineers claimed that negotiation was the activity that was really going on. They recognized the ideas within translation as an interpretation process, but preferred the concept of negotiation because it was thought to much better reflect the social processes that they were familiar with. "Translation sounds like a language teacher thing", as one engineer noted. The idea of the actant was less well received, so after a very brief discussion we settled for a compromise: actors are human beings and actants are technological devices. As noted above, this distinction is not necessarily in accordance with orthodox actor network theory, but workable for our purposes here as the idea of an actant having agency was maintained. This idea – that actants have agency – caused some laughter and a number of jokes were exchanged: "This is exactly so"; "I have often thought of this myself"; "When things get impossible, you think like this – it's like when you are hitting your computer". So even if the vocabulary was altered slightly, the basic idea of the agency of the actant was maintained – maybe there is a ghost in the machine. So far so good: actants have agency and the engineering project is a negotiation process where actors and actants gradually find solutions. In the workshop discussions this became the point of departure, but it turned out that there were some disagreements about the meaning of this.

Different career paths exist in The Company: engineers can choose between being project managers, technology specialists or business managers. Each role aims at different tasks, and it is possible that this could be the underlying reason for different attitudes. The project managers, mostly consisting of younger engineers, were very much in favour of the idea: "This is exactly what we see in our projects"; "We constantly have to negotiate everything"; "Why did they not tell us this at the engineering school?" On the other hand, the technology specialists, mainly older engineers, fully recognized the idea about the agency of the actant, but would not give up on the idea of objective, true and right calculations, plans and ideas. They strongly maintained that there are things that escape negotiations: "You cannot negotiate with gravity", as one of them put it. "There are things that are not up for negotiation". Even if the specialists recognized that engineering projects have an administrative side, they concluded that someone else should deal with that. That could, for example, be project or business managers. The task of the specialists would still be to deliver trustworthy plans, calculations and ideas. A very strong focus on, and attachment to, "the thing itself" for this group is evident here. The third group, the business managers (some with PhDs in production management, and at the apex of the hierarchy within the group), were very eager to promote the idea of agency and negotiation. "Actors, actants and projects – it's all politics", noted one. "Project management is change management. No matter what you do you are changing the organization", related another.

So, here we have two (or maybe three) different interpretations of the results of my analysis from this workshop. Even if these differences in interpretation exist, which they probably do, it turned out that this group could unanimously agree that if all recognize that implementation can be described as a negotiation process (translation), then it should be possible to ease some of the tensions experienced in project implementation. This is progress, and points in the direction of transcending the problematic of the split. The frustration often felt could be dealt with if it is recognized that it is a negotiation process and that actants have agency. Besides this key finding, there are some other lessons to be learned here. It appears that the group management has some work to do in more substantively discussing the work of the specialists and the project managers. This workshop brought some of these problems to the surface, but these discussions are far from over – there is still a long way to go. The specialists' more rigid attitude could, or maybe should, be relaxed somewhat in order to allow them to take on board the full consequences of the insights of the translation alternative. They are, of course, in some way correct that one cannot negotiate with gravity; but during their work, even as specialists, there is plenty of room for negotiation with both actors and actants. This could be about listening to others, entering into dialogue with others – actors and actants – and not just seeking the ultimate truth in their own elegant and rigorous calculations and plans. During our workshop we discussed the difference between "being right" (in Danish *ha' ret*, literally meaning "have the right" or "being right", meaning having or knowing the truth) and "get the right" (in Danish *få ret*, literally meaning "get the right" or "being granted the right" – meaning that others recognize that we/I/you are right). With this distinction, we can see that the specialists run the risk of being right, but that no one else will acknowledge that they are right – which will result in conflict and frustration. In order to reduce or ameliorate such frustration the engineers should see the negotiation process as a way of not only "being right", but also as necessary if they want to "get the right" from others involved in any form of project implementation. This was yet another very notable outcome of the workshop, as the engineers are now able to ask one another whether they just want to "be right" or they also want "to get the right". The latter must be just as important as the former if engineering projects are to stand any possibility of ever being successfully implemented.

What's in it for the Engineer?

When I first asked Jesper and Bjarke about what it is like being an engineer, I got the first story about constructing production concepts and implementation – a very neat story, told many times before by many other engineers, proud of their professional technical expertise. But when I asked them about their everyday lives I got yet another story – a story about troubles, insecurity, negotiations, frustration, success and failure. The differences between the two stories are, hopefully, now obvious; and engineers, and especially engineering schools, could learn from this – as indeed we all could. Instead of expecting implementation of fixed plans to be the right and real way, we should consider the implementation of a plan as a process, and possibly a process of translation. If we recognize this, we – and especially engineers in their everyday practice – could maybe avoid some of this frustration because we would know, and expect, that negotiations, dialogues and often conflicts and power struggles are a necessary, constitutive and unavoidable part of the process. The dialogue with actors and actants in the network is also a real experience.

For this process-oriented approach to become part of the engineer's reality it seems that the engineering schools should consider how they address the implementation process. Being able to make a reasonable and workable production concept is all important to the engineer-to-be, but so is the implementation process itself. In Jesper and Bjarke's everyday lives coordination takes up half their time and this should, as a pragmatic matter of course, be reflected in engineering school curricula. The point here is that this has to be done without jeopardizing the all-important "thing itself" – the engineering part; but it has to be implemented in an integrated way, just as it is in Jesper and Bjarke's everyday practices. There is a difference between being right and getting the right and, as argued here, one plausible way to get the right is to engage in the negotiation process with actors and actants. The workshop group unanimously agreed that recognizing project implementation as a negotiation process (translation) should make it possible to ease some tensions and frustrations. These engineers may now ask one another whether they just want to "be right" or whether they also want "to get the right". Both point us in a pragmatic, and plausible, direction in transcending the problematic of the split – both in real day-to-day engineering life and in engineering school curricula.

For research purposes, there are also many things to be learned here. If Latour (1993) is any way close to being correct that we have never been modern because no split exists between technology and the social in everyday engineering life, as they are co-constructed, then our research should also reflect this fact. Models and process theories may consider the relationships between actors, actants and the language used to describe these processes and relationships. Avoiding naive and static implementation models (which don't work), we need the single narrative that Latour argues in favour of: that is, a narrative that is able to weave together the social, the discursive and the real into a single narrative, thereby transcending the problematic of the split between coordination and "the thing itself".

References

Brown, Steven D. (2002). Michel Serres: Science, translation and the logic of the parasite. *Theory, Culture and Society* 19(3), 1–27.
Bucciarelli, Louis L. (1994). *Designing Engineers*. Cambridge, MA: MIT Press.
Callon, Michel (1986). Some elements of a sociology of translation: Domestication of the scallops and the fishermen of St. Brieuc Bay. In John Law (ed.), *Power, Action and Belief: A New Sociology of Knowledge*. London: Routledge and Kegan Paul.
Harman, Graham (2009). *Prince of Networks: Bruno Latour and Metaphysics*. Melbourne: re.press.
Henriksen, Lars Bo et al. (2004). *Dimensions of Change: Conceptualising Reality in Organisational Research*. Copenhagen: Copenhagen Business School Press.

Jaffee, David (2008). *Organization Theory: Tension and Change.* Boston, MA: McGraw-Hill.

Latour, Bruno (1987). *Science in Action: How to Follow Scientists and Engineers Through Society.* Milton Keynes: Open University Press.

Latour, Bruno (1993). *We Have Never Been Modern.* New York: Harvester Wheatsheaf.

Latour, Bruno (2005). *Reassembling the Social: An Introduction to Actor-Network-Theory.* Oxford: Oxford University Press.

Law, John (1992). Notes on the theory of the actor network: Ordering, strategy, and heterogeneity. Centre for Science Studies, Lancaster University. Online papers. Available at http://www.lancaster.ac.uk/sociology/research/publications/papers/law-notes-on-ant.pdf.

Law, John (1987). Technology and heterogeneous engineering: The case of Portuguese expansion. In W.E. Bijker, T.P. Hughes and T.J. Pinch (eds), *The Social Construction of Technological Systems: New Directions in the Sociology and History of Technology.* Cambridge, MA: MIT Press.

Law, John and Hassard, John (1999). *Actor Network Theory and After.* Oxford and Keele: Blackwell/Sociological Review.

Snow, C.P. (1957, 1993). *The Two Cultures.* Cambridge: Cambridge University Press.

Taylor, Frederick W. (1911, 1998). *The Principles of Scientific Management.* New York: Dover.

Trevelyan, J.P. (2007). Technical coordination in engineering practice. *Journal of Engineering Education* 96(3), 191–204.

Trevelyan, J.P. (2009). *Engineering Education Requires a Better Model of Engineering Practice.* Proceedings of the Research in Engineering Education Symposium, Palm Cove, Queensland, Australia.

Vaughan, Adrian (1997). *Engineering Knight Errant: Isambard Kingdom Brunel.* London: John Murray.

Chapter 5

Coordinating the Repair and Modification of Offshore Production Systems: The Role of the Project Manager

VIDAR HEPSØ

We[1] have over the years followed up the coordination work associated with engineering challenges that involves collaboration across boundaries, i.e. different engineering disciplines and companies. In most of these projects the practitioners involved had to balance the degree of uncertainty of having a highly confirmatory shared syntax vs. handling an increasing degree of novelty and uncertainty. The consequence of this degree of novelty will influence the coordination practices. Confirmatory routine work requires a different approach than a creative problem-solving process. In our situation this field revolves around those customers in an operational setting who need engineering services, whether in the form of modifications and repair vs. those who provide the needed vendor services and competence to modify or repair the customers' equipment. The engineers are organized across boundaries which are partly company internal and partly company external. The work tasks of the engineers are knowledge intensive as they have to diagnose the problem, develop an appropriate solution and manage the actual repair and modification. There is a substantial amount of shared practice that eases this project management process. However, across these situations and boundaries, the

---

[1] The chapter and some of the research was originally a collaboration project between me and Irene Lorentzen Hepsø. She suffered a very bad stroke due to a brain aneurysm in 2011. Irene has since then been in a coma and will, according to the prognosis, remain in that state. In honour of her memory I have chosen to continue using "we" in the text and to keep her visible, but not to include her as a co-author. An earlier version of this chapter was presented by the two of us at the European Group for Organizational Studies (EGOS) meeting in Lisbon in 2010.

engineers have different skills, experience, and professional and organizational identities. In short there will be differences in syntax and interpretations. Some work is routine based, while other activities are more novel. The approach to developing a shared understanding and to approaching a problem will differ across the boundaries. To address this complex coordination challenge, project managers work on behalf of the customer to plan and execute the modification and repair. The situation we address is where the project manager executes his/her role within a dominating syntax. This means that the project manager operates in a space where he/she has the possibility to use this syntactic dominance in the coordination of the other partners.

The structure of the chapter is as follows. We start with the theoretical background, and then describe our research approach. After this we present the case from the Norwegian oil industry. Our research question is therefore how does the project manager enact his/her role having the control of the dominant syntax? After the presentation of the case we analyse the case and some empirical examples in greater detail using the attributes of Østerlund and Carlile (2005). This analysis is the platform to flesh out more in detail the implications of building trust in the coordination of work. To address the power issues associated with trust and the coordination of work we use the distinction between generated trust and façades of trust (Hardy et al., 1998: 78). In the conclusion we summarize our contribution. A list of abbreviations and pictures from the world of subsea oil and gas production is included at the end of the chapter to help the reader who is not familiar with this business.

Theoretical Background

Groups develop coordination mechanisms across boundaries to manage interdependence among individuals, groups, organizational units and activities when confronted by behavioural uncertainty. Traditional coordination literature (Malone and Crowston, 1994) hardly addresses the practices associated with developing a shared understanding through coordination, and presupposes that coordination is a syntactic challenge. Our approach to coordination is founded on theories of practice (Bourdieu, 1977; Giddens, 1979; Orlikowski, 2002; Wenger, 1998; Østerlund and Carlile, 2005, Hepsø, 2008). We are following the practical consequences of action when actors are engaged in activity. The core perspective we lean on are the conceptualizations of Paul Carlile (2002, 2004) that describe the development of knowledge across boundaries through three levels – syntactic, semantic and pragmatic – related to the degree of novelty.

Much work is efficiently coordinated on a syntactic level since we are able to function with a sufficient common understanding of aim, task, problem, solutions, priorities, methods, procedures and language. To ensure communication on a syntactic level is, therefore, a prerequisite for efficient coordination. Established teams working with known tasks within known situations have developed a common syntax and a common practice. Our definition of syntax follows Carlile's (2004: 558) definition as something that defines the relationship between actors at a boundary, a common lexicon that sufficiently specifies the differences and dependencies of consequence at the boundary between actors.

Østerlund and Carlile (2005) have developed a theoretical framework for knowledge sharing in complex organizations. Here they define seven attributes of relational thinking in practice theories: differences characterizing the relations; dependencies characterizing the relation; changes characterizing the relation; identifying the relational forces; blurring category boundaries; specifying the empirical practices; and, finally, historically constituted vs. emerging relations. This framework, with its attributes, is our platform to inform the discussion on the role of trust in the coordination of work.

Coordination mechanisms are ways of working with the problem of interdependence and uncertainty, and represent a logic in which work can be coordinated and information handled. The coming of more knowledge-intensive corporations increases the importance of trust as a coordination mechanism (Adler, 2001; Kramer and Cook, 2004; Lane, 1998; McEvily et al., 2003). If trust exists in the relationships it means that much of the coordination work involved in monitoring and controlling others becomes of less importance (McEvily, 2003: 92–3), and this reduces the transaction costs associated with coordination. The large increase in the number and variety of exchange relations and the increased complexity and uncertainty of the business environment cannot be handled without the presence of interpersonal and inter-organizational trust (Lane 1998). Trust as an organizing principle or mechanism is an important prerequisite for collaboration and coordination of work. The problem with much of the existing research on trust is that it does not make the role of power explicit when analysing trust (Hardy et al., 1998). Power is an important issue in Carlile's model of knowledge creation at a boundary. In the coordination of work across boundaries the nature of collaboration is typically both trust-based and power-based. We now start with the methods and approach.

Methods and Approach

This project has been undertaken within Alpha Oil, a major Norwegian oil company. The first author is an associate professor at Trondheim Business School. Since 1993 she has been connected to an interdisciplinary research centre with main focus on the challenges and opportunities within implementation of technology and health, security and environment (HSE). During the 1990s she studied the work of project managers in the modification of offshore production systems to see how they managed to coordinate work across the organizational boundaries. She was introduced to the setting through two years' close cooperation with the general manager for modification projects at Alpha Oil. He was the senior manager for the project managers who planned and executed modification work. She interviewed about 30 people from different parts of the organization and with different roles in offshore modification projects, and conducted participant observation of work practices for over a month. In this period she had an office in the vicinity of the project managers and observed their coordination activities. The second author is a researcher at Alpha Oil R&D and has worked with organizational development enabled by new information and communication technologies for over 20 years. He has a PhD in anthropology, but petroleum engineering has been his field of study in this period. He is also adjunct professor at the Norwegian University of Science and Technology (NTNU). The particular project of this chapter was set up to sketch future subsea operation and maintenance scenarios at Alpha Oil. A substantial part of this project was to describe the present socio-technical practices within the subsea environment. In 2002 and 2003 the author spent considerable time with subsea engineers in various parts of the company to understand their work practices, to learn the necessary ropes of the ecology, develop personal relations with the insiders, and to earn trust. The work is based on around 90 days of participant observation in the period, daily diaries/fieldwork notes and over 30 interviews with subsea engineers and project managers both inside and outside Alpha Oil. Alpha Oil's internal electronic archives of email communication and Intranet have been used extensively as sources. Several workshops have been held with subsea personnel both in Alpha Oil and among vendors where the case and the findings have been discussed.

Case: Repair of Subsea Systems

The empirical examples we present are from the oil business in Norway (Hepsø, 2008). In the repair and modification of offshore production systems most activities are coordinated within a sufficiently specified syntax. Subsea operation and maintenance cover all activities and interfaces necessary for the execution of subsea work using manned or unmanned intervention, including essential activities in connection with the subsea systems: start-up, operation, maintenance, shutdown and removal of subsea pipelines and subsea systems. A subsea production system is typically connected to a topside installation as satellites, producing hydrocarbons from nearby reservoir pockets. Subsea production systems consist of subsea completed wells; subsea production trees/well-heads; seabed tie-ins to flow-line systems; and control facilities to operate the wells. Such systems are unique when it comes to remoteness in installation, service and operation. There are valves/sleeves that can be remotely operated on the subsea wells to control the amount of produced flow of oil and gas. Now and then these systems break down or they need to be modified to meet new operating requirements (see Figure 5.1). When the study was undertaken Alpha Oil had close to 200 of these subsea wells. To accomplish repair and modification many domain areas are involved: the offshore installation personnel; those responsible for the technical systems onshore; and some external contractors. This domain competence is enrolled from diverse internal organizational units and a pretty diverse group of external companies. The modification team consists of people from several communities of practice (CoPs) across substantial boundaries. People across the boundaries might interpret their task and purpose differently, and their stakes vis-à-vis a project's delivery can also diverge.

The main organizational actors in this setting are, first, the business assets. The business asset is responsible for the operation and maintenance of subsea systems, and is the customer. They have the resources, and plan the work to be undertaken in the subsea domain. Assets have their operational and technical tasks undertaken by subsea engineer coordinators (SECs). They are the project managers in this case. SECs are the technical experts of the subsea equipment; they have the overall responsibility for following up the technical condition of the subsea systems and plan the intervention on non-functioning subsea systems. The SEC represents the customer vis-à-vis the others in the planning and execution of the repair. As such they have to be skilled project managers. SECs work onshore but have frequent communication with offshore personnel, and they spend considerable time offshore on vessels during subsea intervention campaigns. The hands-on and day-to-day operation of subsea equipment is undertaken by the central control room (CCR) operators at the offshore installations. The CCR is the main customer but the SEC is in most cases an intermediary between the CCR and others. When monitoring the oil and gas production in real time, these CCR operators follow up the performance

Figure 5.1   Subsea production systems on the seabed

Note: Above left: subsea production systems on the seabed. Above right: an ROV replaces a subsea control (SCM) module. Middle left: Subsea equipment and ROT on the deck of an intervention vessel. Middle right: intervention vessel launches an ROV. Bottom left: The central control room (CCR) of an oil installation. Bottom right: An offshore oil installation.

of and day-to-day operations of subsea systems. Additional Alpha Oil internal organizational units plan vessel operations and provide engineering support.

In addition to the oil company's internal organizational units, a number of subsea system suppliers do substantial work. Two mechanisms are important in this arrangement. The first, the subsea pool, is a pool of equipment shared between the assets used during intervention on subsea systems. The second, the oil company/Sub-man service agreement (SSA), is a framework contract initiated for technical services and provision of subsea equipment. Subsea suppliers like Sub-man have workshops close to the Norwegian west-coast bases where they repair, overhaul and prepare subsea equipment for installation or replacement. Much of this work is part of the SSA framework contract. Shipping companies provide vessels that are hired on short- or term-long term contracts to execute the intervention work, and the chartered vessels must get hold of the correct equipment before they can start the subsea intervention work offshore. Once the vessel has been mobilized and is intervening subsea, the actual remotely operated underwater vehicle (ROV) or subsea robot operation, installation or repair of the subsea equipment is undertaken by ROV operators under supervision of the oil company and the Sub-man supplier expert on board.

Let us sum up the total operational support for subsea installations. Much of the coordination work is highly confirmatory and can be undertaken using a proper project management and subsea engineering syntax. There is an intricate mix of oil company internal and external actors, where each partner contributes with their key competence. They are chosen because they are experts in their domain, and this fact provides challenges to a highly confirmatory syntax. Heterogeneous professional identities among the parts, large differences in domain competence, the existence of knowledge-intensive coordination tasks and contingencies that develop due to planning and executing intervention work in rough offshore waters move the challenges of coordinating the work out of its highly confirmatory syntax. This forms the back curtain of the challenge that SECs as project managers must handle in trust-building and boundary-spanning activities.

Identity, Community, Skills and Practice of the SECs

In order to enquire into how trust is developed by the project manager within an existing syntax let us recall that the subsea engineering coordinator (SEC) is an obligatory passing point for establishing or re-establishing availability of subsea systems. The SEC of the asset is typically an MSc engineer with valuable experience from various technical disciplines. He or she has typically more than 10 years of operational experience. An SEC has a large network of contacts in the offshore and onshore organization of the asset and among the internal and external suppliers. He or she nurtures contact with the SECs of the other assets for peer assistance and colleague communication. The relationship between SECs is described as easy-going and open. They say they trust each other, and argue that this peer-based trust has emerged naturally in the absence of deliberate attempts or intent to create it. This relationship is what we later refer to as of one of spontaneous trust (Hardy et al., 1998: 78). SECs have responsibility for their separate technical systems, but they have a community of practice relationship among themselves, with high degrees of shared meaning evolved through training, experience and practice. The SECs have reached their positions via learning the tricks and ropes of their discipline in very similar ways. This work is knowledge-intensive in the sense that he or she knows the subsea systems, the constraints on and possibilities of the receiving topside installations. His or her experience normally consists of a general understanding of petroleum and process engineering (i.e. the hydrocarbon flow from the reservoir to the export of the produced gas and fluids). These are the elements in which the subsea systems are integrated. The SEC will also have detailed knowledge related to the construction and parts of the subsea systems.

Describing the Syntax and Coordinating the Work Across Boundaries

It is because of their experience with subsea systems that the SEC is able to diagnose malfunctioning subsea equipment, often in collaboration with control room operators and subsea suppliers like Sub-man. These engineering skills must also be combined with project management, since in addition to diagnosis the coordinator also evaluates the costs related to the replacement of subsea modules. He or she writes the repair procedures for the replacement of the equipment and must "walk the talk" in following up the procedures he or she has written. In doing so, he or she tends to get direct feedback on what works and what does not. Subsea intervention work is an activity that involves numerous human elements both within and outside the Alpha Oil organization. In addition, non-human elements of subsea installations – rigs, vessels, control rooms, choke valves, plugs, control cables, and oil and gas test separators – are elements that link the human resources together (Figure 5.1). The SEC typically develops a diagnosis of the problem together with colleagues onshore and offshore:

Some control room operators want to have my help, others do not, and it is very important how I approach them. I tend to know many of them and how to handle them. If they perceive me as a "Besserwisser", I will have serious problems helping them. This can be a problem because many of them do not have the same detailed understanding of the subsea facility as I have. I must be humble and over time I have earned their confidence and trust. (SEC project manager)

The SEC is keen on presenting himself as a friendly helper and under-communicates his competence in the domain. A control room operator phrased the same relation in the following manner:

The SEC is helping us, there are wonders he can do to find the malfunctions. I have most of my experience from traditional non-subsea platform wells and must admit that I can have problems grasping the full complexity of the subsea systems. When I present the information located in the operator station and discuss the details with him, we have a good dialogue. He suggests things, I click on the buttons and we evaluate the reaction via the SAS system. One by one the potential failure modes are discarded. In most cases the two of us are able to find a solution to the problem we are facing.

An example of such a diagnosis and the proposed action related to this situation in the engineering syntax is as follows: "Subsea electronic module A on well X subsea control module [SCM] suffers from low insulation resistance (short circuit). To rectify the situation the faulty SCM has to be pulled to the surface for repair and replaced with a fresh subsea control module". If the problem is not to be solved by the SEC in collaboration with the CCR, he mobilizes a larger network:

I can make contact with some SEC colleagues in other assets, which I have a lot of contact with and discuss the problem. One of them is sitting nearby. I can contact the subsea engineering service organization or approach suppliers like Sub-man directly because of the SSA framework contract. We often need the supplier of the equipment to handle the specific details of the particular subsea system. The shipping company and marine contractor for ROV-services do an excellent job but I do not know them that much. They are usually contracted for 2–3 years but have little to contribute in this part of the process. We plan and diagnose and the last two parts I mentioned execute. (SEC project manager)

Hearings, mail, telephone or meetings are used where different personnel contribute to this planning process and the development of a scope of work (SOW): other SECs, platform managers, CCR production managers, operators and Alpha Oil subsea support organizations. The SOW document is the primary syntactic tool the SEC uses to involve the disparate actors and coordinate the work. This SOW contains information related to health, safety and environment (HSE): important telephone numbers, contact persons, lines of authority and communication. It addresses:

- the malfunction and the problem to be solved;
- why it should be done in a particular manner;
- the conclusions of the diagnosis;
- asset field information with maps over templates and pipelines;
- the work process sequence during intervention and repair;
- preparations before replacement;
- the replacement process in detail;
- the close-down sequence of the well;
- the module or equipment to be replaced;
- requirements/needs for tools and documentation.

Each SOW tends to have a "cut-and-paste" character since much information can be reused from past interventions. Various actors that participate in the subsea intervention will be able to take out the elements they need to coordinate and execute their part of the work, and it functions as a least common denominator. An SEC argues on the SOW:

> *You must not forget that many of these operations are repeated because it's not the first SCM repair procedure I write. I focus on what I know will be important based on things that have not worked in the past. These procedures cannot be too detailed; the people doing these jobs are experts in their fields. I draw the various elements together into a unity that will work for all participants. (SEC project manager)*

Mobilizing Resources for Eased Coordination of Work

In most assets the SECs do not have the budget for these activities themselves and appeal to asset managers to have the budget released. They must argue why this should be prioritized over other activities. A list of the most urgent subsea interventions legitimated via cost and risk assessments is made by the SECs in collaboration with the logistic planner. This activity also requires a strict standardized method to make each potential intervention comparable across assets. A cost sharing and coordination system has been developed, and this coordination mechanism is important for the smooth execution of subsea operations and maintenance. During campaign mobilization, demobilization and transition costs are shared among the participating parties. This cost structure or principle for sharing and reporting costs was itself a consequence of a compromise between the requirements of different actors in the setting that we will not discuss here. The SECs need to follow up intervention costs on their systems. At the same time, the other participants also need to have a flexible structure that could show their part of the intervention costs, split and aggregation. Other institutionalized hierarchical and market-related coordination mechanisms exist as syntactic resources for the SECs. The subsea intervention tools used are part of the subsea tool pool, formalized via the "detail pool agreement" (DPA). Assets that are members of the tool pool will receive the scope of tools needed in the near future interventions to maintain stable production. For the SEC, the subsea pool and the DPA are resources he or she can use to mobilize the intervention and which he or she needs to get the job done. Fixed prices exist for Sub-man activities via the SSA contract – like the replacement and repair of SCMs, and mobilization and demobilization costs for vessels. These predefined coordination mechanisms are existing resources that can be used or enrolled by the SEC as resources. In many respects this is a syntactic platform that the SEC can take for granted and use his or her resources on coordinating other types of work.

Replacing the Subsea Equipment

The SOW is overall, and considerable articulation work is needed to fill in the details to make the SOW plan robust in use. A SEC reports on the scope of work:

> *The operation should of course in principle be undertaken according to the scope of work. Adjustments must be made and improvisations undertaken to deal with contingencies. The descriptions in the SOW are on a high level because we acknowledge that the participants have*

core competence and are experts in their fields. I focus my details on the interfaces and overlapping work tasks. (SEC project manager)

A typical example of this operation is related to the change of a subsea control module (SCM) on a subsea template (see the bucket above right in Figure 5.1). It is too complicated to address the nitty-gritty details of a subsea control module replacement here, but it requires a delicate collaboration between the SEC, the installation's CCR, subsea vendor Sub-man, shipping vessel crew and ROV operators. Alpha Oil is leading the operation, playing on the other participants' resources and key competence. The SEC is always in charge of running intervention activities on his or her assets well on behalf of the platform and customer. The SEC checks operational logs from the various participants, coordinates the operation and reports the status to the CCR. The CCR is responsible for logging operations (i.e. subsea system valve status, position open-shut on the installation). ROV operators log all their operations. Suppliers like Sub-man always run the intervention equipment. The vessel crew makes sure that the vessel is on the right dynamic positioning (DP) location vis-à-vis the seabed subsea systems and for placing the equipment in the right place on the cargo deck. All participants have continuous communication with the SEC during operations, and the others report to him or her after execution of the intervention activity.

Discussion

We now discuss the case in the light of Østerlund and Carlile's (2005) framework associated with attributes for describing knowledge sharing across boundaries. For many reasons it is easier to start with the sixth attribute of Østerlund and Carlile (2005: 95) – specifying the empirical practices – before we take the other attributes. A description of the practices has already been presented in the previous section of the chapter, and we discuss the coordination of work in relation to Østerlund and Carlile's key questions.

The active unit we describe in this chapter is the SEC. We present the relational qualities of the coordination work undertaken. However, we would like to point out that the SEC is not the only active contributor here. The other groups are not passive participants who just do what the SEC tells them, As a Sub-man engineer states:

I often come up with important hints and feedback since I designed the system some years ago and know it much better than the SEC.

My involvement in a tricky diagnosis is important and can make the difference in coming up with a solution to the problem.

Alpha Oil has also given us assignments to solve some challenges none have worked with before because they know we can do it better than the other vendors in this domain.

What kinds of action are then taken to be analytically central? We focus on the relational trust-building practices of the SECs: their ability to go through with their project by using a highly confirmatory dominant syntax while at the same time handling the management of meaning when being faced by novelty and risk. This is an issue we will soon come back to in greater detail.

What is then the temporal organization of action? Do we talk about short-term moves or long-term enrolment practices? The SEC manages to take advantage of the situation in Alpha Oil, in a setting where the subsea organization of Alpha Oil is a network of internal and external actors. He or she mobilizes a temporary network of independent companies and Alpha Oil subunits through his/her coordination work. The SEC is the main architect that creates the access and the foundation for a temporary structure, or loose coalition of operational and administrative services that come together for a specific business purpose in the asset: to repair subsea equipment. Major parts of this enrolled assemblage disassemble when the purpose or scope of work has been met (i.e. subsea repair executed). This assemblage of human and non-human resources can exist temporally or be more long-lasting in Alpha Oil, but the SEC brings them together in a practical arrangement. Through the coordination of work the SEC is able to align and move the assembly or collective of human and non-human resources in the direction he/she wants: repair subsea systems (Latour, 1987). The focus is short term – meet the project schedule; but it is also a long-term enrolment practice that we come back to when we discuss the seventh attribute.

We now address the other six attributes of Østerlund and Carlile (2005: 93–6) and start with the first attribute: differences characterizing the relation. The main issue is to delineate the differences in the work practices, including knowledge and perspectives. It is important to address the relational and dynamic aspects here since boundaries are flexible and can change. Though practice edges and boundaries can become blurred and grey, people manage to cope with this reality every day. The main difference between the relations described in this setting is that one part has a need and other parts have the competence to meet that need. It is a customer–vendor relationship.

The customer plans and coordinates important parts of the work and is often given valuable input from the others, but the internal and external vendors always execute the work. While the customer is always internal, there are both company internal and external vendors. They form a networked organization in the sense that they are mobilized for a short or longer time period. The networked organization is set up based on core competences, so that each part of the network is doing what it is good at. The consequence is that the relations between the parts of the network are complementary. Each part has a clear and separate identity. Alpha Oil assets and the delegate of the asset, the SEC, want to use this network of groups because they have special skills in doing particular tasks, and therefore have a domain-specific identity. The employees of every partner in the network must identify themselves with the job they are doing for Alpha Oil but also identify themselves with their own company. They work on behalf of Alpha Oil and must comply with the values and the business processes of Alpha Oil. At the same time, they have their own corporate culture, a culture that can be very different from that of Alpha Oil. The life-world of a shipping company is different from that of an oil company. If we look at the work associated with the replacement of a subsea control module, the identity and heterogeneity of the partners remain visible throughout the operational phases of this process. They all work towards a common goal, i.e. replace the SCM; yet in this work they maintain their uniqueness and heterogeneity. The shipping company conducts vessel operation, and remotely operated tool (ROT) operations involving the replacement of the SCM are always done by suppliers like Sub-man. Some of the vendors have membership in different communities, both among the vendors and within the customer organization. This means that they can collaborate one day as partners but be competitors later on. As such they must identify themselves with Alpha Oil when they do work for this customer and show allegiance and identification with another oil company when they work for them. A negotiation of identities is important in this process. The participants are able to handle dual and shared loyalties.

The easiest way to build a common identity in this diverse group is via practice and daily collaboration. It is repeated relevant interaction in practice that fosters trust and identification. The SEC must be confident that this loose organization or network knows Alpha Oil's syntactic work processes (meaning roles, responsibilities for work tasks) and health, environment and safety standards. Without this knowledge it will be difficult for the different organizations to do a good job. At the same time the SEC is dependent on using the core competence of these vendors. The SEC is able to balance these shared and dual loyalties. He or she must enrol them so that they accept the syntax, meaning the values and operating procedures of Alpha Oil. At the same time he or she must let them keep their loyalties to their own organization because their identities tend to be linked to their core competence and practice.

If we look at what are the critical trust elements associated with differences we see several issues. Some elements are more important if we are to understand how the coordination of work is linked to trust. These elements are: potential participation in the community of SECs; core competence related to subsea engineering; company boundaries and identity/allegiance. Seen from the perspective of the SECs there is the most trust in the relationship among SECs. The SEC trusts his/her peers the most. Trust is reduced when moving across company borders and when the technical domain knowledge of subsea engineering becomes more peripheral. In this sense trustworthiness is proportional to the subsea engineering competence, and consequently a reduction in trust occurs when we move from subsea engineering competence to marine and shipping operations. This means that Sub-man share more of the same identity, interests, educational background and domain expertise, and are regarded as more trustworthy than the ship crew doing the intervention work.

The second attribute of Østerlund and Carlile addresses the dependencies characterizing the relations. This dependency is a fundamentally relational phenomenon. A domain expert can only be categorized if there are other expert domains and if the level of competence also differs within the domain, like the relation between expert and apprentice. A vendor presupposes the existence of customers. It is easy to see in our case how the dependencies exist among different elements. All parts are needed to fulfil the mission. Domain knowledge held by different parts is always dependent upon each other. The customer does not have the necessary in-house skills and competence to execute the work, and is dependent upon a networked group of internal and external vendors to undertake the job. The customer plans the job via the SEC, and the internal/external vendors execute the tasks. The vendors need the projects to survive, but also to sustain their role and identity via continuously extrapolating competence and skills. The latter have to participate in the reification processes and negotiate meaning in processes together with the customer and other vendors (Wenger, 1998). The shared notion and understanding of dependency is an important condition for trust. This dependency is not always in balance. Alpha Oil is more dependent on vendors keeping competence in key areas like subsea engineering. Other vendors are replaceable since several competitors deliver more or less the same service, like shipping companies and ROV operations.

The third attribute addresses the changes characterizing the relation. This attribute depicts how particular relations and the differences and dependencies characterizing those relations change over time. Action and practice have an emergent quality. Contingencies develop, and if we want to describe the relation between a customer and a vendor in the subsea domain we have to include the particular direction and character of change found in that relationship. We will not address this attribute in more detail here because this is one of the main topics of the chapter and it is well covered in the other parts of the discussion.

Power is the fourth attribute of Østerlund and Carlile, and power is used to identify the relational forces at play. The ability to control the meaning of the network of actors is in most situations in the hands of the SEC. The SEC is therefore in a prime negotiation position to work with the syntax. As the project manager he/she gets the work done, but also maintains present power structures and minimizes the risks associated with the job. In most respects he or she is the obligatory passage point for the budget and scope of work. The SEC has a clear picture of the structure of network relationships and is helping to recognize opportunities and eliminate duplication through collaboration. The SEC is also skilled and speaks the language of all participants. He or she is always actively involved in coordinating the discussions taking place, and helps manage the give-and-take needed to guide the various actors through the repair process. The SEC facilitates through the SOW the development of a shared notion of interdependence and shared interests. It forces the parts to see that they have to rely upon each other to fulfil their collective interests. Interdependence is an important condition for establishing trust. By getting the parts to realize that they are mutually dependent upon each other, the first steps to trust are taken.

Power is also important in the relationships, and vital to understand action. The generation of trust is a complex, dynamic and continuous process. Trust depends upon signalling trustworthiness in ways that create meaning for others. Sincerity and mutually compatible goals will not suffice if their meaning cannot be demonstrated in action. Hardy et al. (1998) have described four forms of trust. The first, spontaneous, is not handled here because it is mainly developed within a community of practice with a high degree of shared meaning and common practices. This form of trust is not so relevant across boundaries, as mentioned earlier in the chapter. It matches the relationship SECs have with each other. The three other types of trust relevant here in relation to power are generated trust and façades of trust, manipulation and capitulation. Generated trust (Hardy et al., 1998: 81) develops when cooperation is created via management of meaning, and it partly resembles the relationship the SECs have in relation to Sub-man. The latter do not share the same symbols and discourse as that of the peer community of SECs, but shared meaning is constructed via the SEC's coordination of work (i.e. the SOW that is written and through ongoing communication through action during subsea intervention work).

Manipulation (Hardy et al., 1998: 81) is the first façade of trust, where cooperation is power-based but cooperation is achieved through management of meaning. On the surface it is similar to generated trust. The project manager uses symbolic power to reduce risk, increase predictability and calculative benefits, with the consequence that synergy related to collaboration is reduced. Since trust is a risky investment, it should not be surprising if SECs prefer to use power to achieve the necessary coordination in intervention campaigns vis-à-vis the other participants. Even though it may not bring about the creative synergy it increases the likelihood of predictable behaviour. As Paul Carlile (2002) has reminded us, not all the sources of novelty are of value; its value must also be determined. The consequence of this uncertainty of novelty and its value is that counterpart alternatives are reduced, therefore also the synergy in the inter-organizational collaboration. This type of trust also resembles partly the relationship with the subsea vendor Sub-man, but is a complex issue and we will return to this shortly.

Capitulation is the final type or the second façade of trust. This type is also power-based through dependency and socialization, and resembles the trust relationship toward shipping companies and marine operation contractors. These have the skills and competence that can be most easily contracted to other companies and are given two- to three-year contracts with Alpha Oil. These two act more as a tool that works on behalf of the dominant partner, Alpha Oil. The risk to the dominant partner is low, but the synergy is also low. The weaker party is to a larger extent socialized to accept, unquestioningly, its limited room for manoeuvre and does not interfere with the domain of subsea engineering.

Hardy et al. (1998) have given us some ideal types of trust that are important to understand the practices and coordination work of project managers, but in real life these ideal types of trust have shortages when it comes to catching the dynamics of the inter-organizational coordination work we have presented in the case study (Hepsø, 2008). If we look at the relationship between Alpha Oil and Sub-man, the main issue is domain knowledge and skills. Alpha Oil does not possess the core competence to have full manoeuvrability. It is company policy that non-core competence work tasks should be performed by external vendors. Alpha Oil has the critical competence and skills within the technical disciplines of subsea operation and maintenance to be a demanding customer. Alpha Oil's subsea organization does not possess the domain knowledge related to execute marine and ROV operations. It is therefore dependent upon collaborating with external companies that have domain knowledge of Alpha Oil systems and practices, but have core competence in areas where Alpha Oil personnel do not have the skills and expertise. The external supplier needs time to develop this competence, and this does not make it easy to switch vendors. Let us take Sub-man, the main vendor of subsea systems, as an example. Alpha Oil has until the turn of the century mainly had an installed base of Sub-man subsea equipment and must rely on support from Sub-man personnel who know these systems pretty well. This reduces Alpha Oil's ability to use the power that is latent in the relationship. One is not always satisfied with the products and services of the vendor, but dependent upon having a long-term and trustful relationship. In the case of Sub-man the creative synergy is also needed to develop novel features in the next generation of subsea systems.

The SEC must master the paradox of earning the trust of the other participants in his or her coordination activities to get the subsea repair job done. At the same time, the SEC leaves no doubt that he or she is the obligatory passage point; that the other participants involved in the subsea intervention campaign work on the SEC's behalf and according to his or her scope of work. Even though the SEC decreases the hierarchic syntactic control, Alpha Oil still has the operator ship and the responsibilities that come with subsea operations. A certain level of stability, harmony, values, decisions, planning, procedures and goals must be in place in the syntax, while at the same time the SEC as project manager must accept that instability, disagreement, risks, conflict, diverging goals and values exist in the network. These are the requirements the SEC must balance to get the potential out of this loose organization.

The fifth category deals with blurring category boundaries. We have already mentioned the blurred attributes of the networked organization that executes the subsea repair in a previous attribute, and how identity and allegiance change among the actors. In relational process thinking boundaries among categories blur and are in constant change. This means that social systems or the subunits described in this setting are not so easy to divide in parts but form a seamless whole through practice. Trust and power are enmeshed in each other, as mentioned above; but such power relationships tend to be downplayed and a more egalitarian attitude develops between the parties. There is a formalized syntax for trust that functions as a platform for eased coordination of work. The SSA framework contract is one of these institutions, a formalized contract between the oil company and the vendors. It typically describes the expectations, rights and duties of the relationships. In normal operations, formal mechanisms like the SSA tend to be background resources, but are brought forward when disagreements have to be handled. In day-to-day operations the actors work seamlessly, but when work breaks down some of the formal and legal arrangements are brought forward.

Since we have already covered the sixth attribute specifying the empirical practices, we address the seventh and final attribute. This attribute addresses to what extent a practice is dependent upon the historically constituted relations among participants and their unfolding practices, or the emergence of relations in ongoing interaction. Each subsea campaign is short-lived, emergent in nature and temporary. A number of communities that exist separately are mobilized to repair the subsea system. After this work has been undertaken they are demobilized again. However, it is difficult to understand the trust development in the setting without understanding the historically constituted relations. Most of the SECs have a background from the Alpha Oil internal subsea engineering support unit and have worked with all parts of the subsea life-cycle: subsea concept, project development and operations. There are a number of key individuals with subsea domain expertise and long experience that links the engineers together. The special collaboration with Sub-man was originally founded in a contract, but it has enabled both Alpha Oil and Sub-man to fill complementary roles and develop the foundation for a long-lasting relationship. The tight collaboration with Sub-man is the consequence of a joint development of several generations of subsea equipment since the mid-1980s. In this situation, Alpha Oil personnel have had close contact with Sub-man, often sitting in their office facilities during the development of new equipment. Close interaction has also developed during building, testing and deployment of the subsea equipment. Throughout the years, a substantial number of personnel have switched employment from Alpha Oil to Sub-man and from Sub-man to Alpha Oil. The shared syntax is well established in the historically constituted relations.

Coordination of work depends upon the degree of novelty involved. In a situation with a low degree of novelty that makes a highly confirmatory syntax proper, the coordination of work can be undertaken as efficient as possible, exploiting the dominating syntax. Negotiations of syntax and interpretations are as few as possible. In a situation with high novelty and low confirmation an appropriate syntax is not established. Existing syntaxes are developed for situations with institutional properties not equal to the actual situation or task, and will therefore not be appropriate. Proper syntax and interpretations must therefore be developed through negotiations or proper reification and participation. In situations with high confirmation and low novelty trust can be easily institutionalized and accepted through aligning and enrolling a dominant syntax, and often just the two façades of trust (Hardy et al., 1998) are sufficient.

On the other side, in a situation with high novelty, trust is based on shared understanding. This understanding must be built on participation in reification processes that develops the new syntax. To establish this new syntax requires participation in reification processes up and down the semantic and pragmatic levels of Carlile's (2002, 2004) stack model. A kind of generated trust (Hardy et al., 1998) must be developed.

Contingencies emerge when some of the pre-planned situations and responses no longer match the existing syntax. When this type of novelty appears, there is not necessarily a common existing syntax that can be used to handle the novelty across the boundary. Still, for the project manager in our case the challenge is to sustain the proper amount of syntax and deal with the emerging novelty. The SEC has to balance the work with deliverables and customers that should ideally be clear, transparent and highly confirmatory on one side. On the other side more novel and less confirmatory challenges should also addressed to take out the learning and innovation potential from the project participants' capabilities. If the project manager follows a regime of too strict and syntactic control he/she will not be able to take out the full potential of the subcontractors and harvest the consequences of potential emergent learning and innovation processes in the ongoing work.

The goal for the coordination of work will differ depending upon the situation. Is the objective to provide high confirmation, predictability, speed and quality of planning and execution, or is it to provide a creative synergy for novelty and innovation? We asked how the project manager enacts his/her role when having control of the dominant syntax. Traditional coordination theory covers the most important issues regarding challenges in coordination of work where a clear and precise division of labour is important. He or she can either trust that those responsible fulfil their roles and their tasks in a proper way or develop routines to follow up their practices. Still, there is always an element of power associated with the trust we have described. When new situations develop that cannot be placed in the existing division of labour and the existing syntax at the boundary, we see from our case that the problem of novelty can be met in two ways.

First, find one responsible actor to deal with the novelty on behalf of the others, have trust in the part and hope that it works. The networks of actors involved in subsea repair are experts in their domain and the coordination of work is based on the core competence of the partners. Sub-man has developed numerous novel solutions for Alpha Oil over the long time period the two companies have collaborated. In the case study we presented how the SEC described the overall syntax in the SOW, but not the details. He let the various actors develop their novel parts of the work, but made sure to coordinate the interfaces between the actors. As such he was exploiting a façade of trust that was enabled by the existing division of labour and coordination practices. To keep the common syntax on an aggregated level and letting the actor decide on their own how to execute the task only works when the actor's activity can be clearly marked and need not engage in novel coordination work across boundaries with other actors. Trust can compensate for the lack of shared syntax as long as the boundaries are pretty clear and aligned with an existing division of labour.

Second, develop shared understanding and shared syntax through negotiation and reification/participation (Wenger, 1998). This resembles generated trust, something that develops when cooperation is created via management of meaning, through negotiations across boundaries – whether within or between communities of practice. Hardy et al. (1998: 69–70) argue that trust can be conceptualized as a communicative, sense-making process that bridges disparate groups. This approach emphasizes the shared meanings that partners use to signal trust and trustworthiness to each other: "Trust is therefore an inter-subjective social 'reality' that cannot exist, regardless of the good intentions of partners, unless the symbols used to signal trustworthiness have meaning for all parties". Hardy et al. (1998: 75) argue that the existence of sincerity and mutual goals will not generate trust unless partners can communicate with each other.

The second option requires movement up and down the semantic and pragmatic levels in Carlile's (2002, 2004) stack model before they can agree upon a new syntax for collaboration across boundaries. It will require substantial coordination of work and transaction costs among the many actors. However, if the first option is feasible, the project manager can be the mediator and boundary spanner black-boxing or translating the novelty into a syntax that the whole network of actors accepts. He or she can also use power to sanction the new syntax. This is an option that the project manager will stick to as long as possible when he or she has control of the dominating syntax – not so surprising since novelty need not always bring added value. However, the dominant syntax of the project manager might be challenged by two conditions: first, in a situation with a high degree of novelty, where the project manager might lack the appropriate syntax for the task. He or she also knows that the other actors are not in possession of the appropriate syntax due to the novelty of the situation. The other condition is that one of the actors in the network of subsea repair has so much power vested in their domain competence that they are able to challenge the syntax of the project manager.

For the practices of the project manager, the conclusion is the following. In the first option the challenge is to facilitate the façades of trust. However, in the second option the project manager must facilitate the negotiation of meaning and development of a new shared syntax in an attempt to achieve generated trust.

Abbreviations

CCR: Central control room – a room with operators who control the production process on an oil and gas installation.

DPA: Detail pool agreement – the agreement that describes the day-to-day operations of the subsea pool, including its products, services and the rights/obligations of the pool partners.

Sub-man: An acronym for a major manufacturer and service provider of subsea equipment.

HSE: Health, safety and environment.

ROV: Remotely operated vehicle, used for inspection and repair of subsea systems.

ROT: Remotely operated tools – tools used for replacement of heavy subsea components.

SCM: Subsea control module – a subsea component that contains important control functions of a subsea system.

SEC: Subsea engineering coordinator – engineer responsible for delivering availability of subsea systems; the project manager in this study.

SOW: Scope of work – the description of the subsea intervention work to be executed.

SSA: A framework contract between Alpha Oil and Sub-man that eases the delivery of subsea services.

Tool pool: A pool that gives its partners eased access to subsea intervention tools and reduces the life-cycle costs of tool ownership.

References

Adler, P. (2001). Market, hierarchy, and trust: The knowledge economy and the future of capitalism. *Organization Science*, 12(2), 215–34.

Bourdieu, P. (1977). *Outline to a Theory of Practice*. Cambridge: Cambridge University Press.

Carlile, P.R. (2002). A pragmatic view of knowledge and boundaries: Boundary objects in new product development. *Organization Science*, 13(4), 442–55.

Carlile, P.R. (2004). Transferring, translating, and transforming: An integrative framework for managing knowledge across boundaries. *Organization Science*, 15(5), 555–68.

Giddens, A. (1979). *Central Problems in Social Theory: Action, Structure and Contradiction in Social Analysis*. Berkeley, CA: University of California Press.

Hardy, C., Phillips, N. and Lawrence T. (1998). Distinguishing trust and power in interorganizational relations: Forms and façades of trust. In C. Lane and R. Bachmanm (eds), *Trust Within and Between Organizations: Conceptual Issues and Empirical Applications*. Oxford: Oxford University Press, 64–87.

Hepsø, V. (2008). "Boundary-spanning" practices and paradoxes related to trust among people and machines in a high-tech oil and gas environment. In D. Jemielniak and J. Kociatkiewicz (eds), *Management Practices in High-Tech Environments*. Hershey, PA: Information Science Reference, 1–17.

Kramer, M.R. and Cook, K.S. (eds) (2004). *Trust and Distrust in Organizations: Dilemmas and Approaches*. New York: Russell Sage Foundation.

Lane, C. (1998). Introduction: Theories and issues in the study of trust. In C. Lane and R. Bachmann (eds), *Trust Within and Between Organizations: Conceptual Issues and Empirical Applications*. Oxford: Oxford University Press, 1–30.

Latour, B. (1987). *Science in Action: How to Follow Scientists and Engineers through Society*. Cambridge, MA: Harvard University Press.

McEvily, B. et al. (2003). Trust as an organizing principle. *Organization Science*, 14(1), 91–103.

Malone, T.W. and Crowston, K. (1994). The interdisciplinary study of coordination. *ACM Computing Surveys*, 26(1), 87–119.

Orlikowski, W.J. (2002). Knowing in practice: Enacting a collective capability in distributed organizing. *Organization Science*, 13(3), 249–73.

Østerlund, C. and Carlile, P. (2005). Relations in practice: Sorting through practice theories on knowledge sharing in complex organizations. *The Information Society*, 21(2), 91–107.

Wenger, E. (1998). *Communities of Practice: Learning, Meaning, and Identity*. Cambridge: Cambridge University Press.

Chapter 6

Role of the Virtual Team Leader: Managing Changing Membership in a Team

KAJA PRYSTUPA-RZĄDCA and DOMINIKA LATUSEK-JURCZAK[1]

Introduction

Virtual teams are a popular team formation for cost-effective and efficient conducting of various activities across the globe. Most commonly, they are defined as a group of people sharing common goals virtually, where at least two members are situated at different locations (Hinds and Mortensen, 2001). Distance between them may range from being located at different offices to being located on different continents (Hinds and Mortensen, 2001; Malhotra et al., 2007). Despite positive aspects of virtual teams, such as cost reduction and faster product delivery, this new organizational structure has brought many challenges that may hamper its effectiveness. Virtual teams are more prone to conflicts (Hinds and Mortensen, 2005) as the traditional mechanisms of socialization are missing (Townsend et al., 1998). As a result, they strive with weak interpersonal bonds, unshared context and poor information sharing (Hinds and Bailey, 2003; Hinds and Mortensen, 2001).

Various researchers indicated that leadership is a crucial factor for ensuring virtual teams' efficacy (Berry, 2006; Pauleen, 2003; Vroman and Kovacich, 2002). Skills required for successful management of virtual teams are more complex than those skills required for leading face-to-face teams (Berry, 2006; Maznevski and Chudoba, 2000; Nicolson et al., 2007). Hence, the role of the virtual team leader is more challenging as it requires knowledge and understanding of team dynamics, regardless of time, space

---

[1] The project was financed by funds from the National Center of Science upon decision no DEC- 2011/01/N/HS4/04414.

and communication differences between virtual and traditional work environments (Dyer et al., 2007). Relying merely on technology causes various coordination problems (Cramton, 2001). Moreover, in a virtual environment it is hard to develop and maintain trust, which is vital to a team's ability to manage effectively decision processes (Jarvenpaa and Leidner, 1999; Witchalls et al., 2010). Virtual team members are more prone to so-called focus drift, and they tend to be less satisfied with their interaction than members of co-located teams (Straus and McGrath, 1994).

In virtual teams the membership is often fluid and changes according to task requirements (Townsend et al., 1998). Often team members are employed in the middle of the project to perform particular tasks, and after their completion they depart. In such circumstances, it is difficult to maintain the team's cohesion. Moreover, virtuality hampers the socialization process, which is important for the maintenance of the team's efficiency (Townsend et al., 1998). From this perspective, the issue of changing membership emerges as a serious challenge for the team's leader to overcome. Notwithstanding this, in the literature devoted to virtual teams this important issue has been neglected. Therefore, the purpose of this exploratory study is to fill the research gap by discussing the question of the leader's role with respect to changing membership in a virtual team.

The first part of this chapter presented a preliminary analysis of prior research devoted to a comprehensive understanding of the leader's role in virtual teams. In the subsequent section the authors will examine whether those findings are conclusive in cases of teams with changing membership and whether their leader played any additional role in managing the introduction of new team members to the virtual team.

Literature Review

Prior research indicated that the role of the leader in the virtual environment is more demanding and time consuming, as the leader should spend 50 per cent more time on managing the virtual team than in the case of a co-located one (Dyer et al., 2007). This has been attributed to various tasks that lie in the scope of the team leader's responsibility. To organize literature review findings, the authors established two distinguishing areas: one pertaining to project implementation and the other pertaining to the social aspects of team dynamics (Figure 6.1).

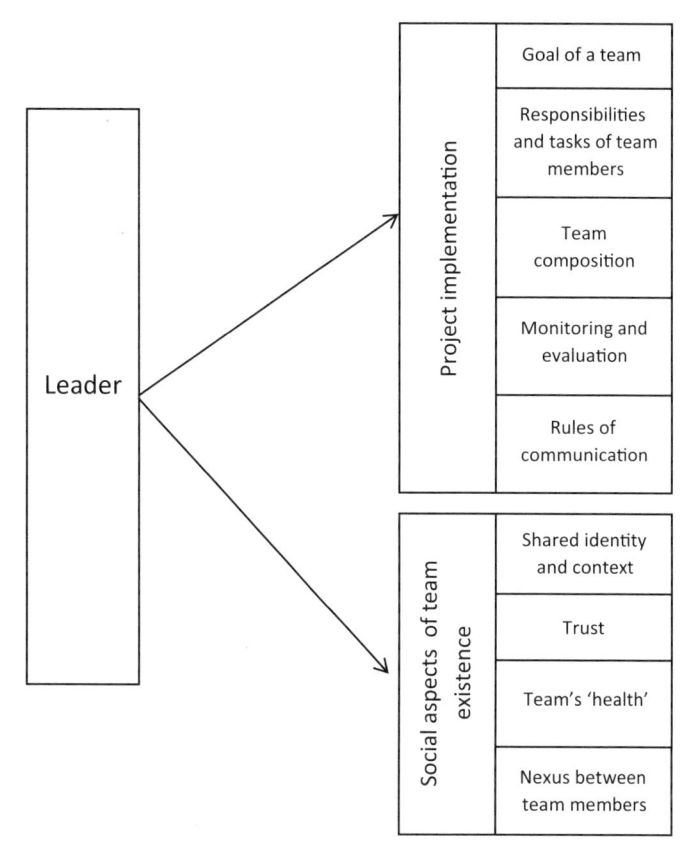

Figure 6.1 — Role of the leader in virtual teams

Leader → Project implementation:
- Goal of a team
- Responsibilities and tasks of team members
- Team composition
- Monitoring and evaluation
- Rules of communication

Leader → Social aspects of team existence:
- Shared identity and context
- Trust
- Team's 'health'
- Nexus between team members

TASKS OF THE LEADER: PROJECT IMPLEMENTATION

In the project implementation tasks, primarily the leader has to define the general goal of a team and the level of virtuality needed to achieve it (Hertel et al., 2005). Awareness of the goal is more important in a virtual environment than in a traditional one due to difficulties stemming from working on target from distance (Kirkman et al., 2002). Afterwards, the leader should develop an appropriate recruiting procedure (Blackburn et al., 2003; Hertel et al., 2005) and identify necessary skills required for achievement of the team's purpose. The main criteria of selection should be: professional/technical knowledge, skills, abilities and expertise (Hertel et al., 2005). Team members should possess such values as self-management, virtual communication, cultural sensitivity, trust-building and skills to use information technology (Blackburn et al., 2003). Those are important conditions because they reduce the number of potential conflicts in the team that are caused by a virtual environment.

Upon a virtual team's launch, the leader has to divide subtasks in a way to reduce coordination of efforts (Hertel et al., 2005; Kayworth and Leidner, 2002). This task determines whether there is high or low interdependence between members. High task interdependence has many positive effects, such as faster development of team cohesion, trust and feeling of contribution to the team (Kirkman et al., 2002). Especially, at the beginning of cooperation, it may reduce the time of "getting to know each other". Low interdependence, in contrast, may cause conflicts that may lead to inefficiency (Hertel et al., 2005).

The leader also has to introduce monitoring and evaluation processes. These are critical matters for any team (Malhotra et al., 2007; Berry, 2006), but in virtual teams they may appear problematic (Townsend et al., 1998). Naturally, managers are unable to observe team performance physically due to the limitations of the virtual environment; therefore, they need to introduce tools that allow them to gather information about the constantly changing situations in the team setting. There are two ways of monitoring the progress (Malhotra et al., 2007):

1. Analyse the electronic discussions and posted documents (asynchronous communication).

2. Analyse the participation in virtual meetings and instant messaging (synchronous communication).

Members facing rapid feedback cycles work more efficiently than those with limited contact (Cramton, 2001). Procedures should allow for early leadership intervention when problems arise.

In designing a future virtual team, the most effective and the most available means of communication should be selected (Horwitz et al., 2006; Kayworth and Leidner, 2002; Oertig and Buergi, 2006; Witchalls et al., 2010). Prior to this decision, the leader has to evaluate the team's situation in several dimensions: nature and type of team; the team's goal; experience in working in a virtual environment; and team members' access to and competency with technology (Duarte and Snyder, 1999).

Despite the importance of regular reliable access to the internet for virtual work, such reliability is not easily available everywhere. The leader has to acknowledge such limitations (Pauleen, 2003). Moreover, communication preferences as well as cultural norms of social interactions should also be taken into account (Witchalls et al., 2010). Maznevski and Chudoba (2000) found out that, in effective teams, the level of the decision-making process was connected to the richness of the communication medium. The team's simple information was transmitted through quick emails, faxes and phone calls. Issues that were more complex were solved within the virtual team via phone calls and conference calls.

Moreover, the leader has to set clear rules for the usage of communications tools; with the increased number of possible ways of transmitting information, the possibility of conflict accelerates as well (Malhotra et al., 2007; Witchalls et al., 2010). Regulations should regard such areas as, for instance, response time or information about absence, which should mitigate the danger of perceived silence. Lack of immediate response from co-workers is particularly dangerous in a virtual team, as it is perceived as an unwillingness to accomplish the work (Cramton, 2001) and hampers the creation of trust (Henttonen and Blomqvist, 2005).

TASKS OF THE LEADER: SOCIAL ASPECTS OF TEAM DYNAMICS

The final category of leader responsibilities is managing the social aspects of team dynamics. Virtual teams often gather individuals who have had no previous relations with each other. Considering the relations within global virtual teams, this structure is even more complex as team members need to understand and communicate effectively under cultural differences, norms and group expectations. Shared identity and shared context are crucial for the team's effectiveness because they mediate potential conflicts (Hinds and Bailey, 2003; Hinds and Mortensen, 2001, 2005). However, the physical distance between people hampers the creation of feelings of closeness and integrity. When shared context is missing, problems are often exacerbated.

Another challenge in virtual environments is the development of trust, as traditional time-related socialization is missing (Townsend et al., 1998). However, the leader should enhance the process, as it is critical to a team's ability to manage decision processes effectively (Jarvenpaa and Leidner, 1999; Witchalls et al., 2010) and decreases the costs of project coordination (Blomqvist et al., 2001).

Various researchers indicated that, at the beginning, all team members should meet face to face (Duarte and Snyder, 1999; Henttonen and Blomqvist, 2005; Lipnack and Stamps, 1999). Introductory meetings enable members to develop relations between each other, which are essential to the fulfilment of the group's mission (Horwitz et al., 2006) and initiate trust development among members (Henttonen and Blomqvist, 2005). Problems are easier to solve when people know who is 'on the other side of the line' (Oertig and Buergi, 2006). However, in practice, only limited numbers of teams expend time and resources to meet physically.

The leader often acts as a nexus between team members (Duarte and Snyder, 1999). In such cases, each employee works from a different location and only the leader communicates with everyone – and only the leader possesses complete information. To increase group connectedness, the leader should ensure that everyone is regularly updated about the project's progress (Brake, 2006) and others' contribution to the work (Hinds and Mortensen, 2001). When such reports are missing, some employees may feel isolated, which may lead to conflict and decreased productivity.

During later stages of the virtual team life cycle, the leader must monitor the progress of the work and the 'team's health' (Horwitz et al., 2006). In case of any problems, the team leader should act immediately, as negative feelings can spread easily among team members, affecting productivity and trust (Brake, 2006).

This literature review found that a team leader should perform most leadership tasks during the initial phases of the team's existence. In comparison, later the leader's role is usually limited to monitoring progress and using managerial techniques to motivate employees. In most research (*inter alia* Blackburn et al., 2003; Henttonen and Blomqvist, 2005; Hertel et al., 2005), the team life cycle approach is applied to management of a virtual team. Changing membership interrupts its continuity, which has not been taken into account by researchers. However, circumstances disrupting team cohesion are not exceptional (Townsend et al., 1998). Therefore, this intriguing issue of a leader's role in managing changing membership in virtual team requires deliberate examination.

Method

The presented case is a part of a two-year fieldwork focused on the dynamics of the work of game development companies. Researchers introduced an interpretative qualitative approach based on grounded theory (Glaser and Strauss, 1957; Konecki, 2000) and a case study method (Yin 2003) to examine the leader's role with respect to the changing membership in virtual teams. According to the latter, the choice of the unit of analysis is subordinated to the purpose of the research. Hence, it is not random, but instead is the result of a conscious selection process. The case of Cubicon is informative for analysis of leadership in virtual teams for several reasons. Firstly, game development requires close cooperation of team members, and the achieved result is a combination of work of different specialities: art designers, game designers, programmers and music composers (Zackariasson and Wilson, 2012). Thus, frequent communication and the development of common understanding of conception are necessary for its successful completion. On the other side, in a virtual environment of nonverbal communication, which favours understanding the meaning of conversation that is missing (Vroman and Kovacich, 2002), it is more difficult to retain contextual information (Henttonen and Blomqvist, 2005). Among examined organizations, only a few decided to conduct their projects virtually. Secondly, the Cubicon team serves as an example of a group of co-workers, most of whom never met physically as they were located in different countries all over the world. Only the team leader and the co-founder of the organization maintained face-to-face interactions. Therefore, the case allowed researchers to examine the consequences of the virtuality in its full spectrum. Lastly, Cubicon's team faced various challenges stemming from the virtuality of the workplace, such as *inter alia* group socialization, development of trust and setting up of rules of communication.

The basic techniques of data collection were semi-structured interviews with team members and analysis of the company's blog and forum. Blogs are particularly useful in qualitative research as they allow researchers to examine social processes over time, having insights into the everyday life of the team members (Hookway, 2008).

The interviews were conducted in the period April–June 2012 and the documents used in the analysis were from the period 20 November 2006–29 July 2012 (around 450 pages of documentation).

Data was coded and analysed with software dedicated to qualitative research. To maintain credibility of results, the author used the data triangulation method, which allowed for the development of dominant themes of research.

The identities of the interviewees as well as described products that appeared in the article were changed according to agreement between the researcher and the organization under study.

Results

This paper presented the study of the work of Cubicon, a small indie[2] game development studio which established a virtual team for its project development.

Greg Grudziński, the founder of Cubicon, was a young but experienced game designer. Having published his first game, *Wizzardy*, at the age of 18, he later worked at one of the biggest game development studios in Poland and then at smaller one as well. Despite being successful at work, Greg had been developing his own product after hours, a sequel to *Wizzardy*. He created an online gamers' community around his game, and through it he became acquainted with other people who shared similar ambitions. In mid-2011, Greg decided to pursue his dreams by launching Cubicon with his colleague from a previous project, Lena Czerwona, a talented graphic designer. Having developed a general idea for the game design, Greg started assembling a team for the project execution.

SELECTION OF TEAM MEMBERS AND PROJECT LAUNCH

While preparing the plan for project implementation, Greg estimated that to be able to complete the project he needed to employ additional personnel. Lena was responsible for graphics while he looked after design and programming. However, taking into account other obligations associated with running a business, Greg was not able to manage the whole burden of programming. Moreover, the game needed a soundtrack and neither of them was experienced in this field. After analysis of the project's schedule, he decided to employ two specialists: a programmer and a music composer.

Through years of professional experience in the games industry, Greg had developed many contacts, both locally and internationally. Having a large pool of potential co-workers, he chose two people to join his team. The first one was Uwe Andreassen, a Norwegian programmer who became acquainted with Greg through an online community devoted to *Wizzardy*. They already had a chance to work on one project. The other specialist hired, Bob Eastman, was a British composer who had also worked with Greg earlier and had maintained contact with him through the gaming community. Therefore, Greg's decision

---

2 Indie (from independent). The notion developed in the 1990s in opposition to studios that were producing games for funds received from international publishers, and thus they needed to consult them on every decision. Indie game developers became visible on the market with the growing popularity of online and mobile gaming.

to select Uwe and Bob was based upon expert knowledge, self-management and trust developed through collaboration with them.

ORGANIZING THE WORK

Game development is conducted mostly according to the agile project development model, where work is divided into milestones. For each milestone, employees are given a particular task to accomplish, and later they are accountable for them. Division of tasks and responsibilities stems from the area of expertise of each employee. At the beginning of the project, the team leader outlined only general tasks to perform, as the implementation preceding a subsequent milestone is given more detail (Zackariasson and Wilson, 2012). Following this methodology, Greg prepared a set of tasks for each team member to perform within the given milestone. Interdependence of tasks between employees varied. In game development, each scene is a result of the work of designer, programmer and graphic designer. Usually, the programmer and graphic designer need to work simultaneously, exchanging finished pieces of work. Hence, the tasks performed are rather highly interdependent. While dividing tasks between team members, Greg tried to create a situation where there was high interdependency between each team member and their work, and lower interdependency between team members themselves. For instance, he performed those tasks that required frequent cooperation with Lena, as he could easily meet with her physically. The smaller parts of the code were delegated to Uwe, and later were adjusted into his code. Bob's work was conducted completely separately and was implemented into the product at the end of the project. Following such a strategy ensured high efficiency of game development, which is vital for a game's success as market trends are dynamically changing.

Project implementation with division into milestones allowed introducing the monitoring and evaluation process. Greg tried to deliver immediate feedback to each team member after receiving his or her individual work contributions. This enabled monitoring of project progress, and it was an indication to the employees whether or not they were following the Greg's appropriate direction.

Greg did not introduce any formal regulations concerning usage of communication media. All team members were well experienced in virtual communication as they were using it on daily basis in other projects. The most common form of interaction was email, as it was a preferred means of interaction. The experience of collaboration with team members prior to project launch allowed Greg to recognize each member's preferred style of communication and adjust it to the project framework. However, issues that were more complex were decided over Skype. Greg often contacted Uwe and Lena individually, usually on a daily basis. In comparison, collaboration with Bob required less frequent contact. There were no cases of silence between team members. Each team member was working hard on task accomplishment and in case of problems immediately contacted the team leader. Greg reinforced the habit of swift response to team members, which he introduced while he was collaborating with members of a forum about *Wizzardy*. Such behaviour was accepted as the team's norm. During interviews team members frequently mentioned this rule as being of significant value in virtual collaboration.

DEVELOPING TEAM SPIRIT

Members of the Cubicon team had no chance to meet with each other face to face due to financial reasons and time constraints. Moreover, they had little or no contact with each other prior to the project launch. Lena knew no one except for Greg, whereas Uwe and Bob had exchanged comments a few times through the *Wizzardy* forum. Greg was the only one who knew everyone prior to the project launch. Hence, he acted as the nexus between team members. Interestingly, the whole team has never met physically, even after project completion. Only Greg and Lena conducted regular face-to-face meetings with each other. Uwe visited Poland only once in order to meet with Greg, and it was long before the project. Contacts of Bob met only virtually with him. However, team members were able to maintain group effectiveness, which was possible due to a few reasons. First, as all of them were engaged in the gamers' online community, they operated with a similar language and experience drawn from gaming experience. Therefore, they were able swiftly to develop a shared context. The initial team bonding was strengthened through communication via forums and social media. After completion of each milestone, Greg was informing all team members about the project status to increase connectedness and prevent demotivation.

TURMOIL IN THE VIRTUAL TEAM

As the team was working hard for several months on the project, Greg realized that he had not had enough time to write the game's dialogues, which were indispensable as the game was supposed to be based mostly on dialogue between characters. Team coordination, cooperation with the online community and marketing activities took up most of his time. Moreover, he had no previous experience in the area of the visual novel[3] and dialogue writing, which vaguely influences potential game success. Hence, he decided to look for someone who was well experienced in this area and could not only write narratives but also share valuable market knowledge. Moreover, as the game was supposed to be published in English, the requirement was high language proficiency. As the visual novel market is of rather limited size and most of the productions are developed for a Japanese audience, the list of possible writers was short. Meanwhile, one of the most famous writers in the sector, Yoko Siu, volunteered to join the team. Greg followed a similar selection procedure to the one conducted initially. As Yoko was well experienced in visual novel writing and English was her native language, she perfectly matched the team selection profile. Having no information about her self-management and virtual communication skills, however, Greg assumed that if Yoko had completed several successful projects she possessed those abilities. Moreover, she was well known by gamers and she could attract her fans to purchase the game. As Yoko was living permanently in United States, they maintained mostly email contact. At the beginning, the cooperation seemed promising. However, after a few months of work Yoko started to respond less frequently to emails, and finally she stopped maintaining any contact. Initially, Greg thought that she was preoccupied with different responsibilities.

Greg tried to connect with Yoko virtually, but unsuccessfully as he had only her email and Skype details. For a time he was able to redesign the project timetable, which enabled other team members to work on the project. However, after three months of silence, team members started to become impatient. Finally, Yoko replied and her answer was even more intriguing as she was surprised that not one of the team members knew that during her absence there was a convention season in the United States, which she participated in.[4] She was able to send some parts of dialogues for the game swiftly. Greg decided to give her another chance, as he believed that her absence was only a misunderstanding. However, other team members remained more sceptical. Yoko was unable to regain the others' trust, especially as she proved to be inefficient in her work. As Lena recalled:

> *She said that she writes 3,000 words per day and it's in her opinion a lot. I checked and when I write a post on the forum, it often has 2,500 words, and I do it in an hour. So how she can be so famous and an excellent writer when she can write only 3,000 words per day?*

---

3   Visual novels are interactive fiction games with developed narratives, which resemble mixed-media novels.
4   The convention involved engaged gamers playing as a part of competition.

Greg was also not pleased with the results. Due to Yoko's prior absence, the whole project was delayed by at least three months. He was in doubt about her ability to make a successful contribution to the team. He had limited financial resources and a very limited list of potential candidates. Yoko seemed uninterested in the project's completion.

Through the team's decision, cooperation with Yoko was halted, and Mike Borski, a young psychology student and friend of Lena, filled the position. He had no experience in visual novels; however, he was eager to participate in the project. Moreover, Greg and Lena could meet with him face to face anytime. English was not his native language, however, so the team decided to send the later script to a proofreader. This time, Greg devoted significant attention to the inclusion of the new team member, which was motivated not only by his prior situation with Yoko but also by his awareness of Mike's scant experience in the games industry. The team members who had no chance of physical contact with Mike were sceptical at the beginning; however, they swiftly discovered that he was reliable and accepted him as a team member. Collaboration with Mike was very fruitful and enabled completion of the project. There were some small drawbacks caused by Mike's lack of experience in game development and immense time pressure, which was stressful for him. However, Greg could interact with Mike physically and was able to motivate him more efficiently.

Discussion

In general, prior studies neglected to study the leader's role in the context of changing membership in a virtual team. Addressing this gap, this study's research concentrated on this important issue. The results revealed that the leader plays a vital role in the introduction of a new team member, and that lack of understanding of this necessity may lead to negative consequences on a team's performance.

Interestingly, prior to the appearance of a new team member, the leader successfully fulfilled his role. Analysis of the initial stages of a team's existence confirmed the results of prior research on the role of the leader in a virtual team. The leader fulfilled his duties in both areas: project management and social aspect of team dynamics. Being aware of challenges induced by virtuality, the leader devoted a lot of effort to creating bonds between team members. For instance, Greg knew that high interdependency might lead to conflict (Hertel et al., 2005). Therefore, he divided subtasks in a way to minimize the chance of it and to enhance gradual development of trust. He interfered in team dynamics as a nexus joining separated parts (Duarte and Snyder, 1999). He introduced a rapid feedback principle, being aware that silence may hamper the creation of trust (Henttonen and Blomqvist, 2005). Moreover, he tried to link personal with organizational goals to strengthen motivation of team members, knowing that in the virtual environment awareness of the goal and understanding of its importance are crucial, as distance may hamper accomplishment of the target (Kirkman et al., 2002). Additionally, he introduced a participatory decision-making process, allowed team members to interact more often and enhanced further development of trust (Henttonen and Blomqvist, 2005). As a result, at the beginning the team was working efficiently and without major delays. However, when a new team member appeared, the leader did not adequately work for the inclusion of her within the team. He mostly concentrated on task-related aspects of her work rather than on enhancing the socialization process in the team. In respect to his role in the area of project management, he followed similar criteria of team member selection, division of tasks and goal delivery. On the contrary, in respect to social aspects of team dynamics, he was less engaged in the development of bonds with the new team member than initially he was with others, as he was preoccupied with other tasks. Effective communication and retaining contextual information in asynchronous computer-mediated communication environments tends to require a great deal of effort (Straus, 1996). As a result, when the leader noticed problems appearing during cooperation with Yoko, he did not react immediately, as he was not sure whether they were stemming from cultural differences or from her personal characteristics. Greg did not want to cause unnecessary misunderstandings, which are common in virtual teams (Pauleen, 2003). On the other hand, lack of reaction to the delays was a signal of their acceptance.

Facing a crisis, team members easily turned away from the new member, which was not surprising as they never treated Yoko as a part of the team, sustaining the notion of 'us' versus 'her'. When her behaviour started to delay their work, they rejected her as a team member. Later events proved that they remained hostile even after she delivered some delayed parts of her work. In effect, they made the collective decision to fire her from her work.

The leader took lessons from the case, paying more attention to social aspects of cooperation than relying merely on expert skills, while employing another dialogue writer. He was aware that, due to time constraints, it was more efficient to employ someone with whom he could interact physically. The socialization process occurs faster in a traditional environment than in a virtual one (Townsend et al., 1998), which was vital for the team's morale and project realization. Moreover, in physical circumstances the leader can monitor project realization more easily (Malhotra et al., 2007).

The leader deliberately presented rules of work to the new team member, Mike, leaving little room for assumptions. As a result, he and the other team members could receive a rapid response on whether or not Mike was able to act in accordance with them. Thus, they developed *swift trust*, which allowed them to complete the project as a team (Meyerson et al., 1996).

Lastly, the new dialog writer possessed other qualities: credibility and personal recommendation from one of the team members. Prior research suggested that virtual team leaders were reluctant to use the full potential of the virtual environment by employing people from all over the world, and they preferred to rely on personal recommendations (Pauleen, 2003; Witchalls et al., 2010). The case of Cubicon may serve as the explanation for such a tendency. Virtuality provides limited possibilities for evaluation of candidates. Gestures and facial expressions present in the physical environment are important because they aid understanding the meaning of conversation (Vroman and Kovacich, 2002). In virtual teams, where interactions are limited and time is constrained, it is safer to employ individuals with references, especially in the middle of the project.

Conclusions

The research presented has brought forward an important indication as to the role of the leader in a virtual team with respect to changing membership. It revealed that the issue was neglected by prior studies as well because practitioners insufficiently regarded it. This study proved to be of great importance in this matter and presented the consequences of the neglect of prior research attention. This study's research outlined areas requiring the special attention of the team leader to lead a successful virtual team, such as, *inter alia*, social aspects of time dynamic, setting rules of project implementation or introduction of new team members. The results of this study found that virtuality impaired the life cycle approach to virtual team management; it showed that the cycle may be interrupted by changing membership in the team. Therefore, future research should develop a more dynamic approach, considering changing membership in the virtual team. Further studies also should aim to develop the best practices for a virtual team leader's role in this respect.

References

Berry, G.R. (2006). Can computer-mediated asynchronous communication improve team processes and decision-making? Learning from the management literature. *Journal of Business Communication*, vol. 43, no. 4, 344–66.

Blackburn, R., Furst, S. and Rosen, B. (2003). Building a winning virtual team: KSAs, selection, training, and evaluation, in C.B. Gibson and S.G. Cohen (eds), *Virtual Teams That Work: Creating Conditions for Virtual Team Effectiveness*. San Francisco, CA: Jossey-Bass, 95–120.

Blomqvist, K., Kyläheiko, K. and Virolainen, V. (2001). Filling the gap in traditional transaction cost economics: Towards transaction benefits based analysis using Finnish telecommunications as an illustration. *International Journal of Production Economics*, vol. 79, no. 1, 1–14.

Brake, T. (2006). Leading Global Virtual Teams. *Industrial and Commercial Training*, vol. 38, no. 3, 116–21.

Cramton, C.D. (2001). The mutual knowledge problem and its consequences for dispersed collaboration. *Organization Science*, vol. 12, no. 3, 346–71.

Darling, J.R. and Nurmi, R.W. (2009). Key contemporary paradigms of management and leadership: A linguistic exploration and case for managerial leadership. *European Business Review*, vol. 21, no. 3, 201–14.

Darling, J.R., Heller, V.L. and Wilson III, B.J. (2012). The key to effective organizational development in times of socioeconomic stress: A case focusing on leadership responses to communication challenges. *European Business Review*, vol. 24, no. 3, 216–35.

Duarte, D.L. and Snyder, N.T. (1999). *Mastering Virtual Teams: Strategies, Tools, and Techniques that Succeed*. San Francisco, CA: Jossey-Bass.

Dyer, W.G., Dyer, W.G. Jr and Dyer J.H. (2007). *Team Building: Proven Strategies for Improving Team Performance*. San Francisco, CA: Wiley.

Glaser, B. and Strauss, A. (1957). *The Discovery of Grounded Theory: Strategies for Qualitative Research*. Chicago, IL: Aldine.

Henttonen, K. and Blomqvist, K. (2005). Managing distance in a global virtual team: The evolution of trust through technology-mediated relational communication. *Strategic Change*, vol. 14, no. 2, 107–19.

Hertel, G., Geister, S. and Konradt, U. (2005). Managing virtual teams: A review of current empirical research. *Human Resource Management Review*, vol. 15, no. 1, 69–95.

Hinds, P. and Bailey, D. (2003). Out of sight, out of sync: Understanding conflict in distributed teams. *Organization Science*, vol. 14, no. 6, 615–32.

Hinds, P.J. and Mortensen, M. (2001). Conflict and shared identity in geographically distributed teams. *International Journal of Conflict Management*, vol. 12, no. 3, 210–38.

Hinds, P.J. and Mortensen, M. (2005). Understanding conflict in geographically distributed teams: The moderating effect of shared identity, shared context and spontaneous communication. *Organization Studies*, vol. 16, no. 3, 290–307.

Hookway, N. (2008). 'Entering the blogosphere': Some strategies for using blogs in social research. *Qualitative Research*, vol. 8, no. 1, 93–113.

Horwitz, F.M., Bravington, D. and Slivis, U. (2006). The promise of virtual teams: Identifying key factor in effectiveness and failure. *Journal of European Industrial Training*, vol. 30, no. 6, 472–94.

Jarvenpaa, S.L. and Leidner, D.E. (1999). Communication and trust in global virtual teams. *Organization Science*, vol. 10, no. 6, 791–815.

Kayworth, T.R. and Leidner, D.E. (2002). Leadership effectiveness in global virtual teams. *Journal of Management Information Systems*, vol. 18, no. 3, 7–41.

Kirkman, K., Rosen, B., Gibson, C., Tesluk, P. and McPherson, S. (2002). Five challenges to virtual team success: Lessons from Sabre Inc. *Academy of Management Executive*, vol. 16, no. 3, 67–79.

Konecki, K. (2000). *Studia z metodologii badań jakościowych*. Warsaw: PWN.

Lipnack, J.S. and Stamps, J. (1999). Virtual teams: The new way to work. *Strategy and Leadership*, vol. 27, no. 1, 14–19.

Malhotra, A., Majchrzak, A. and Rosen, B. (2007). Leading virtual teams. *Academy of Management Perspective*, vol. 21, no. 1, 60–70.

Maznevski, M.L. and Chudoba, K.M. (2000). Bridging space over time: Global virtual team dynamics and effectiveness. *Organization Science*, vol. 11, no. 5, 473–92.

Meyerson, D., Weick, K.E. and Kramer, R.M. (1996). Swift trust and temporary groups, in R.M. Kramer and T.R. Tyler (eds), *Trust in Organizations: Frontiers of Theory and Research*. Thousand Oaks, CA: Sage, 166–96.

Nicolson, D.B., Sarker, S., Sarker, S. and Valacich, J.S. (2007). Determinants of effective leadership in information systems development teams: An exploratory study of face-to-face and virtual contexts. *Journal of Information Technology Theory and Application*, vol. 8, no. 4, 38–56.

Oertig, M. and Buergi, T. (2006). The challenges of managing cross-cultural virtual project teams. *Team Performance Management*, vol. 12, no. 1/2, 23–30.

Pauleen, D.J. (2003). Leadership in a global virtual team: An action learning approach. *Leadership and Organization Development Journal*, vol. 24, no. 3, 153–63.

Straus, S.G. (1996). Getting a clue: The effects of communication media and information distribution on participation and performance in computer-mediated and face-to-face groups. *Small Group Research*, vol. 27, no. 1, 115–42.

Straus, S.G. and McGrath, J.E. (1994). Does the medium matter? The interaction of task type and technology on group performance and member reactions. *Journal of Applied Psychology*, vol. 79, no. 2, 87–97.

Townsend, A.M., DeMarie, S.M. and Hendrikson, A.R. (1998). Technology and the workplace of the future. *Academy of Management Executive*, vol. 12, no. 3, 17–29.

Vroman, K. and Kovacich, J. (2002). Computer-mediated interdisciplinary teams: Theory and reality. *Journal of Interprofessional Care*, vol. 16, no. 2, 159–70.

Witchalls, C., Woodley, M. and Watson, J. (2010). *Managing Virtual Teams: Taking a More Strategic Approach*. Report of the Economist Intelligence Unit. Available at: http://graphics.eiu.com/upload/eb/NEC_Managing_virtual_teams_WEB.pdf [accessed 12 March 2012].

Yin, R.K. (2003). *Case Study Research: Design and Methods*. Thousand Oaks, CA: Sage.

Zackariasson, P. and Wilson, T.L. (eds) (2012). *The Video Game Industry: Formation, Present State, and Future*. New York: Routledge.

Chapter 7
Decision Support Systems as Knowledge Workers

ALEKSANDRA PRZEGALIŃSKA

My project is devoted to "genealogical" and structural analysis of decision support systems dedicated mainly to businesses and their influence on work relations within the knowledge economy. I would like it to be understood as a genealogical and structural analysis of decision support systems (DSS) dedicated to business. As a case-study I would like to refer to the Moral Knowledge Expert System (MKES) designed and elaborated by two Polish engineers, Marek Borzestowski and Marek Waszczyk, in "Moral Knowledge Expert System: On the Borderline between Business Ethics and New Technologies" (2005: 1). I will focus mainly on the source of moral presumptions that underlay procedures of the expertise performed by DSS, as well as potentialities and frictions that emerge in the logic of designing such types of DSS as this particular one. Obviously, this DSS is fairly old, however newer types also retained similar architecture. Therefore, MKES can still serve as a good model for analysis.

In general, decision support systems create a set of tools that are supposed to recognize human commands, simulate human expertise and eventually solve problems while learning and referring to the knowledge provided by human beings. Their main contributions are planning, decision making, monitoring, diagnosis and training based on "if-then" inference rules. DSS serve the management, operations and planning levels of an organization (usually higher- and medium-level management) and help make decisions, which may be rapidly changing and not easily specified in advance.

The actual application of DSS went through several phases: model-driven, data-driven, communications-driven, document-driven (also known as knowledge-driven) and, finally – most advanced and broadest – web-based. Currently, the outcome of all those applications is a distinction between two approaches to supporting decision making. The descriptive approach is based on the assumption that the most reliable method of dealing with complex decisions is through a small set of normatively sound principles of how decisions should be made. The second approach, called normative, aims at building support procedures that "imitate" human experts. The most prominent members of this class are expert systems that are based on rules elicited from human domain experts that imitate reasoning of a "rational" human expert. Expert systems are expected to have human attributes in order to replicate human capacity in ethical decision making. They are very flexible and deal well with complex problems by means of applying heuristic methods and ad hoc reasoning schemes. However, they often lack soundness and formal guarantees of results, a problem that we will come back to several times.

Recently, expert systems have gained significance as a tool applied for managing various business areas, such as accounts, finance, controlling, retailing, human resources management, health care systems, customer relation management and e-retailing. Along with natural language processing systems and neural networks, they are constantly improved in order to become ethical leaders of professional bodies. As Bernie Brenner argues, ethical judgement expert systems are or may be able to guide managers through various ethical considerations relevant to ethical decision making and, what is more, assist in developing "their own ethical judgement skills" and improving their "right-decision-making" practices (2002: 86). By establishing and reinforcing "good ethical decision-making practices, training programmes and decision-making tools are also believed to reduce the incidence of "self-consciously unethical decision-making" (2002: 86). Whether and to what extent this is actually possible and desirable is either considered science fiction or a matter of serious ethical concern.

Omar Khalil wrote, in "Artificial Decision-Making and Artificial Ethics: A Management Concern", that expert systems' lack of human intelligence, emotions and values impedes their capabilities of estimating the overall state and hardship of conditions under which the decision is being made, and, what is more, may incorporate intentional or accidental bias (1993: 123) Also, Daniel Dennett (1986: 141) has justly argued that expert systems can pose a significant moral threat to people, causing serious dislocation of familiar work patterns and interactions and impeding our ability to pursue what he calls a "good life". Since the exact topic of this chapter is rather oriented on analysing the meaning of such notions as "ethical judgement skills" and "good ethical judgement decision-making practices", and not responding to these relevant questions, we shall leave them aside. However, we wish to mention that there always emerges one extreme difficulty in confronting such wide and just claims with particular examples of ethical DSS, since the calculus of benefits and harm of each system significantly differs, and the very existence of different ethical theories means that these factors may be accounted for in different ways. Most expert systems are equipped with three basic elements:

1. knowledge database – which includes appropriate facts and rules vital to understand form and solve a problem;

2. inference engine – known as the system's brain, which is a computer program responsible for the methods of inference based on information from the database as well as formulating answers; in the process expert system it uses two-valued, many-valued or fuzzy logic;

3. interface – a computer program equipped with tools to facilitate the communication between system and users (see also Borzestowski and Waszczyk, 2005: 4).

The first two first elements will be of particular interest for us, since our aim is to understand how moral knowledge is embraced and black-boxed within a system such as MKES. Taking into account the fact that the core of the system consists in selecting a moral category, I will make an attempt to reconstruct the assumptions concerning what is and what is not a moral act according to the system and analyse how the data establishing moral knowledge is collected, processed, synthesized and displayed. The particular nature of the architecture of expert systems, especially those most advanced like MKES, is based on taking into account the problem solver's point of view and deploying the choice mechanism (such as test procedures and creating sub-goals) used by the problem solver during his interaction with a complex environment. In other words, unlike the approach that consists in "studying the choice or strategy that the agent ought to use objectively in order to maximize the likelihood of finding optimal solution" (Cordeschi, 2008: 226), the attention here is shifted towards the study of choice that the agent "normally uses" (2008: 226) insofar as the choice is conditioned by his own subjective view of the environment in which he is operating and, what is more important, about which he customarily has only limited information. What is particularly interesting in the context of my considerations is the fact that we are dealing with an ethical judgement expert system that, like most ethical DSS, is based on the so-called normative approach, but is essentially not normative. On one hand, it is designed to serve as an ethical guideline (clearly, it is not purely descriptive), where the risk of suboptimal choices needs to be minimalized; but on the other, it is supposed to be psychologically and neurologically realistic. For this very reason the idea behind ethical judgement expert systems in many respects may seem a *contradictio in adjecto*, for it is self-limiting to such an extent that defining failure or error within it may become an irresolvable problem – an issue we will come back to in the course of our inquiry. However, before I discuss the problems of the internal constraints of the logic of MKES, I will try to trace how such kinds of systems as MKES came into being and what sort of human needs they were primarily supposed to respond to.

Background

> *These were the war years and goal-seeking missiles were literally much in the air (W. Grey Walter, in* Artificial Life, *1997: 37).*

On 25 November 2008 Cornelia Dean published an article in *The New York Times* entitled "A Soldier Taking Orders from Its Ethical Judgment Center". The article was based on an interview with Dr Ronald C. Arkin, who was designing software for battlefield robots under contract with the US Army. Currently, Dr Arkin is mainly preoccupied with designing robot drones, mine detectors and sensing devices which are already common on the battlefield, but his dream is to construct "battlefield assistants" – true robots operating autonomously without any human command post. It may come as a shocking idea, but in fact it is not new at all. Introducing systems that model decision-making and problem-solving processes, and command robots serving and fighting on the battlefield instead of human beings is a very well-established project of post-war Western history. It attracted much attention in the period following World War II, in particular in the 1950s and 1960s when new ideas concerning thought, action, command and control were elaborated under the name of a new, broad discipline: cybernetics. Already by the end of the war there emerged a powerful prescriptive theory of rationality that responded to the needs of that time. This huge shift was obviously a consequence of the idea that "advanced" and "threatened" parts of the world needed perfect protection and, thus, required adequate models of the processes of choice, planning and problem solving to be implemented in industry, government and military agencies. Indeed, the birth of cybernetics in 1943 cannot be detached from the reformulation of ideas of defence and security. As Roberto Cordeschi notes: "it is no coincidence that during the cybernetics era the predictor of an automatic anti-aircraft system is the most frequently mentioned example of a self-controlling and purposive device" (2008: 220). Theory of choice, theory of games and operations research (OR), all embraced by cybernetics, were developed in order to become a remedy to act and choose when information is uncertain. As Philip Mirowski argues in "Cyborg Agonistes", already in wartime "physicists and their allies participated in the reorganization of science patronage and management by coming up with a novel *theory of organization* inspired by physics and (latterly) development of the computer" (1999: 686). The main source of hope was operations research, which was the workshop where "postwar relationships between natural scientists and the sate were reconfigured, and the locus where economics was integrated into this scientific approach to government, corporate management and society" (1999: 690). Thus, the "new rationality" consisted in the idea that prediction and comparison of values, effectiveness and costs of a set of proposed alternative courses of action involving man–machine systems, together with the language of information and control elaborated by cybernetics, may eventually emerge as perfectly adequate disciplines of understanding, explaining and, what is most important, projecting the world. As Andrew Pickering (1995: 31) claims:

> *cybernetics took computer-controlled gun control and layered it in an ontologically indiscriminate fashion across the academic disciplinary board – the world, understood cybernetically, was a world of goal-oriented feedback mechanisms with learning. It is interesting that cybernetics even trumped the servomechanisms line of feedback thought by turning itself into a universal metaphysics, a Theory of Everything ... a cyborg metaphysics with no respect for traditional human and non-human boundaries.*

There are two theories of human processes, developed in the context of cybernetics and early artificial intelligence (AI), which are particularly interesting in the context of Pickering's remarks. The first one, coined by Donald McKay, concerned self-organizing systems; the second one was of Allen Newell and Herbert Simon and is commonly known as information processing psychology (IPP). Both McKay's and Newell/Simon's theories are significant due to the fact that among all early cybernetic concepts they are most sensitive to epistemological problems of higher cognitive processes, such as decision making and choice (in particular when information is incomplete), as well as attention, complex problem solving and consciousness. They were also based on the use of artefacts as models of processes and mechanisms (self-organizing systems in the case of McKay, and computer programs in the case of IPP). McKay introduced the study of these processes by extending the original behaviorist definition of "adaptativness" and "purposefulness" (see also Cordeschi, 2008: 220–21). IPP found its basis in the revision of theory of choice, a topic shared also by theory of games and OR. However, the main idea was to reject the behaviorist conception of human organism as a collection of black boxes that can be mimicked in purely functional terms (a dream seemingly never to be achieved by cybernetics). Instead, their actual specific physical composition was considered irrelevant. What mattered as crucial to explain adaptive and purposive forms of behaviour through negative feedback was the internal organization and structures they shared (McKay, 1956: 30–31). In the above-cited passage Pickering mentioned servomechanisms; and, in fact, a self-guided missile is one of the simplest instances of such kinds of systems as identified by Norbert Wiener. Reformulating the problem of shooting down planes in terms of communication, Wiener and his circle hoped to establish a perfect defence system. Thus, the idea behind such systems was to eliminate any discrepancy between the "symbolic representation" of the "perceived state" and the "symbolic representation" of the "goal state" (Cordeschi, 2008: 220–21) and to represent a possibly wide range of states "from a self-guided missile chasing an aircraft to a man chasing a solution to a crossword puzzle (McKay, 1956: 34). As Orit Halpern argues in "Dreams of Our Perceptual Present":

> *the fundamental premise of these mathematical communication models was that the specific mechanism of any entity did not matter. Only two things mattered: (1) what actions an object took in response to a communicative exchange with another entity units system, and (2) the prediction of future behaviors from the accumulated data of previous interactions (2005: 287).*

In other words, homogeneity replaced difference: "symbolic representations" of the agent and the target were undividable. The effort to compute human action developed "a new attitude toward the enemy, where the Enemy 'Other' and the self behaved the same" (Galison, in Halpern ibid.). Having this in mind, we can easily see that post-war cybernetics truly was an overwhelming metaphysical project which affected all disciplines that were developing dynamically at that time. As Herbert Simon argues (1986: 33): "the past forty years have seen widespread applications of these theories in economics, operations research, and statistics, and through those discipline, to decision making and business". However, business was still far behind, even though the above-described advances in the 1960s laid the foundation for many new business-oriented ideas, including DSS. It was during the 1970s that DSS really took off, with the arrival of query systems, what-if (if-then) systems, rule-based software development and packaged algorithms. At that time the whole framework of rules, domains, heuristics and generative systems was first introduced and implemented. Data and action rules together comprised a generative system with the potential (at least in principle) to generate every location within the conceptual framework. The post-war idea of modeling decisions started to be perceived purely in terms of programming: decomposing and formalizing them as logical problems. Scientists distinguished three basic components of decision models: preference – usually ordinal (which is viewed as the most important concept of decision making process); decision options (usually enumerated); and, finally, uncertainty about the result (Druzdzel and Flynn, 2002). In other words, choice and decision making rested on the clear assumption that a good decision is one that results only from a good decision-making process. And yet, there were no guarantees about the final outcome.

Foreground

In this part of the chapter we will mainly focus on the internal structure of Moral Knowledge Expert Systems (MKES). The main idea of the authors of MKES is to "apply faculties of the worldwide Internet web as well as the concepts being developed in knowledge management with regards to moral problems present in economy" (Borzestowski and Waszczyk, 2005: 1). Since the main purpose of the system is to "enable users to learn about the consequences of moral choices before making them", first we would like to discuss the overall ethical/moral foundations of the project. The authors are attempting to find the theoretical grounds for such an approach, which proved difficult due to the fact that it refers to two seemingly different sources: "Socrates' knowledge search" about good and evil as a basis for virtue; and "utilitarianism" that defines good as maximizing the sum of intrinsic value or minimizing the sum of intrinsic disvalue. Borzestowski and Waszczyk claim that, theoretically, the difference between these two ethics is not as big as it appears to be. It is true that Socrates' ethics refers to the virtue idea as a permanent state of the "soul" (which here, apparently, equals "mind") to perform "good deeds". However, according to the authors of MKES, Socrates left some area to utilitarian interpretation of his concept while building his definition of virtue as possible to learn. Referring to G.E. Moore's *Ethics* (1966), they argue that according to both Socrates' and the utilitarian concept, a person who has a sufficient amount of their own and other people's experience is able to choose good, independently from the frequency, intensity and rationalization of an act by social habits. Thus, the sense of knowledge about good, therefore, lies in the ability to build appropriate argumentation. The main assumption behind this thread of thought is that the criterion of just and unjust choices depends on its complete consequences (Borzestowski and Waszczyk, 2005: 3). Another source of MKES as an idea is finding that the basic problem of prescriptive ethics is the fact that theoretical justification for moral choices remains within a narrow circle of specialists. Despite that, the "moral choice" acts do not openly refer to ethical theories. They are an effect of "current events consideration", "own experience" and "advice of other people either from close or distant circles" (2005: 3). Thus, the web-based expert system that they design is supposed to serve as "an open, universal communication platform" (2005: 3). Taking this into account, already at this point we can indicate two relevant problems:

1. Questions of ethics and morality are not distinguished from one another.

2. A relation between morality and communication clearly exists, but the nature of this relation remains very complex.

In fact, there is much confusion concerning usage of the terms ethics and morality. What kind of role is MKES supposed to fulfil in relation to these terms? Should we, according to its name, place it in the "realm" of morality? And if so, is it supposed to serve as a code of conduct which is held to be authoritative in matters of right and wrong, one which would be espoused by all rational people, under given conditions? Or is it supposed to establish an ideal code of conduct ascribing clear moral value to certain deeds – such as "bribery is always and in every circumstance immoral" – by means of expanding database and meta-level self-observation? On the other hand, some features of MKES – such as addressing questions of how a moral outcome can be achieved in a specific situation and estimating the value – suggest "ethical" understanding of its procedures. This issue remains unsolved.

Now, as far as architecture of (almost) all advisory expert systems is concerned, a key process is the acquisition of knowledge – knowledge that is unstructured and often difficult to verbalize. As we have said before, expert systems use "knowledge" assembled on computers for solving problems that require expert knowledge. An adequately designed expert system imitates the way of thinking of a specialist in a field. Thus, the acquisition of knowledge is in the hands of knowledge a engineer who structures and formalizes it through a dialogue with one or many specialists in a field (see Figure 7.1). However, since knowledge engineering involves broad knowledge "acquisition, demonstration, verification, explanation and maintenance" (Borzestowski and Waszczyk, 2005: 6), the "best candidate" to perform all these duties cannot possibly be a human being. Thus, the "virtual knowledge engineer" is a computer program, ensuring knowledge acquisition from the experts without face-to-face contact.

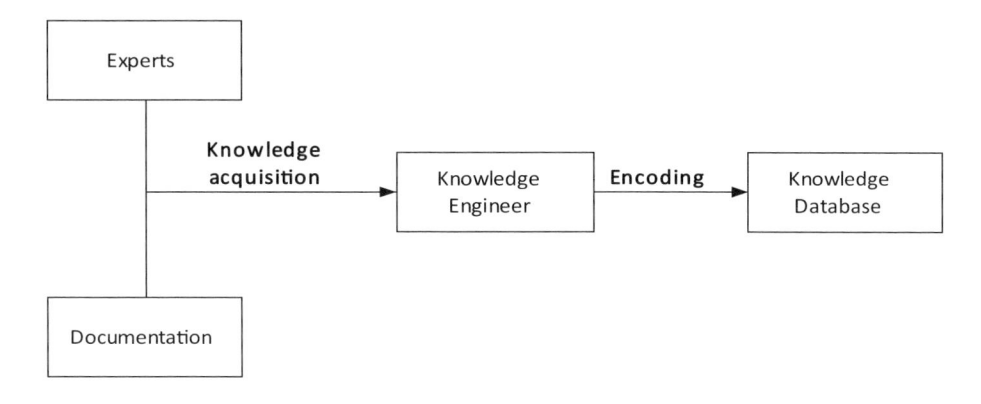

DECISION SUPPORT SYSTEMS AS KNOWLEDGE WORKERS 105

Figure 7.1 Knowledge acquisition

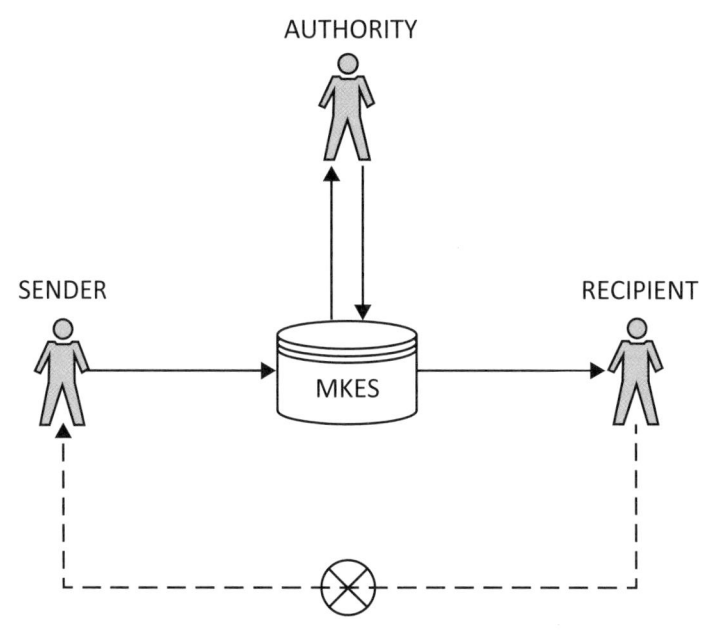

Figure 7.2 Sender and recipient

When knowledge is already encoded as a database, MKES is ready to perform its duties. The idea of MKES divides four elements of the system according to certain roles that we may consider "social": collecting and data processing system (CDPS); senders (S); recipients (R); and authorities (A) – see Figure 7.2. The main function of the CDPS is categorizing of information, namely collecting

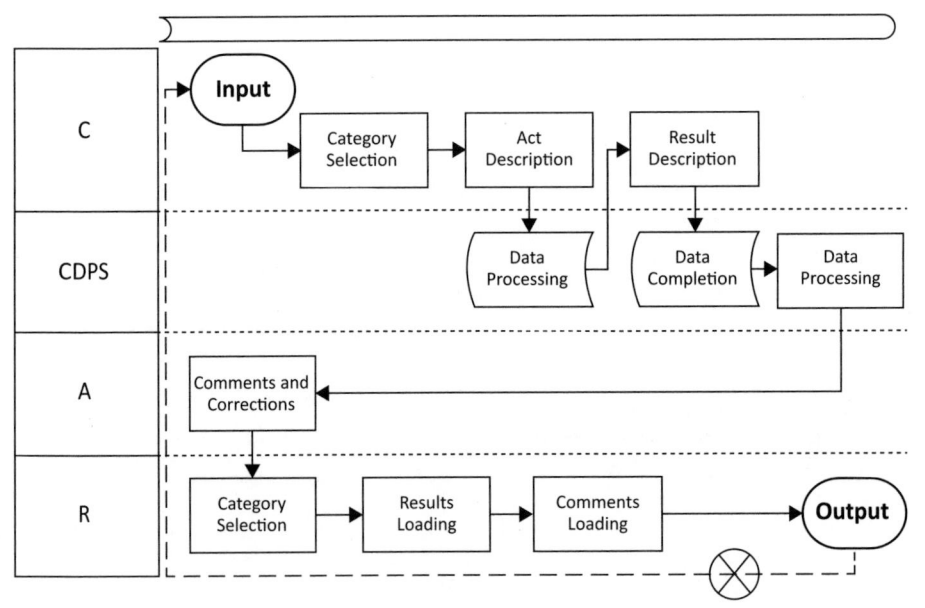

Figure 7.3 Input to output

and storing it in appropriate categories. We will focus on this crucial aspect in the following passage. Senders (S) are to deliver information about moral decisions and their consequences; and recipients (R) are to ask the opinion of MKES before making a moral decision. Authorities (A) are to look after substantial "correctness of results". Thus, we see here a "social organization" that is based on defining, double-checking, feedback and command. Category selection process means to define certain parameters. The first step consists in elimination of those activities that do not have a moral character. The next one is to describe a "moral act" and to insert data into the database. Describing of consequences, as the following step, can happen later and may be a subject to redefinition. The MKES processes the data, generating a synthetic report that is again verified by authority A (see Figure 7.3). The process is complete when entering the system of R, who, having selected a category, reads the comments and can then become S straight after having shared his experiences, restarting the process. Borzestowski and Waszczyk provide the following example of how the procedure is executed by MKES:

> As the first one, the kind of conduct should be stated: passive, where one abstains from acting despite having the knowledge, for example about employees who discard dangerous waste – hazardous for the environment, but profitable for a company; and active, i.e. making a

decision of transporting the waste to the forest rather than to a waste dump. The next parameter is the selection of decision: manager, if it is a disposition; or staff, it is within the competence of an employee. The decision can also be of internal kind, regarding owners, management or employees. There can also be decisions of external kind if it concerns co-operators, competitors or local society. Finally, an act must be selected (bribe, fraud, forgery, etc.) (2005: 10).

As we already know, MKES, like all other expert systems, is by definition not fully informed about the environment. In the course of the activity involving the gradual reduction of discrepancy between the environment and itself, MKES is assisted by the memory of its past activity. Then it selects the input patterns that are closest to the desired one and eliminates others (see Figure 7.4).

As we have mentioned, the role of the authority (A) is to administrate the system and "ensure lack of wrong results" (Borzestowski and Waszczyk, 2005: 7). However, all the rejected and selected patterns represent the internal symbolic vocabulary of MKES. Thus, the only solution is that MKES is limited to a statistical prediction concerning future activities – that is, concerning the probability of evoking certain subsequent patterns. In fact, the system's "beliefs" are defined on the whole by the so-called "matrix of transition-probability" (see also Cordeschi, 2008: 225). Thus, there are serious doubts as to whether we can actually refer to any philosophical-moral system, in particular to utilitarianism, which by its nature is an open system. And even if in the future MKES may work to a certain extent as a probabilistic, self-organizing system that could be possibly equipped with self-observational ability, however, just like any kind of working model it is purely based on analogy, and is bound to break down by showing or lacking properties possessed by the process it was supposed to imitate. Both of these threats are highly plausible, especially within a system that executes "moral" judgements. After all, the only objective justification within MKES of how moral capacity or moral agency develops, and what its nature is, is black-boxed in the system of inputs and outputs. Yet again, like in servomechanistic systems, there are only two things that actually matter: the actions that the system took in response to a communicative exchange with the Senders, Receivers and Authorities; and the prediction of future behaviours (Halpern, 2005: 287). This makes MKES performance accountable only in terms of visibility of its own successes. When it runs efficiently, its internal complexity and its internal shortcomings vanish from sight. Thus, paradoxically, as Bruno Latour (1999) would have put it, the more the system succeeds the more opaque and obscure it becomes.

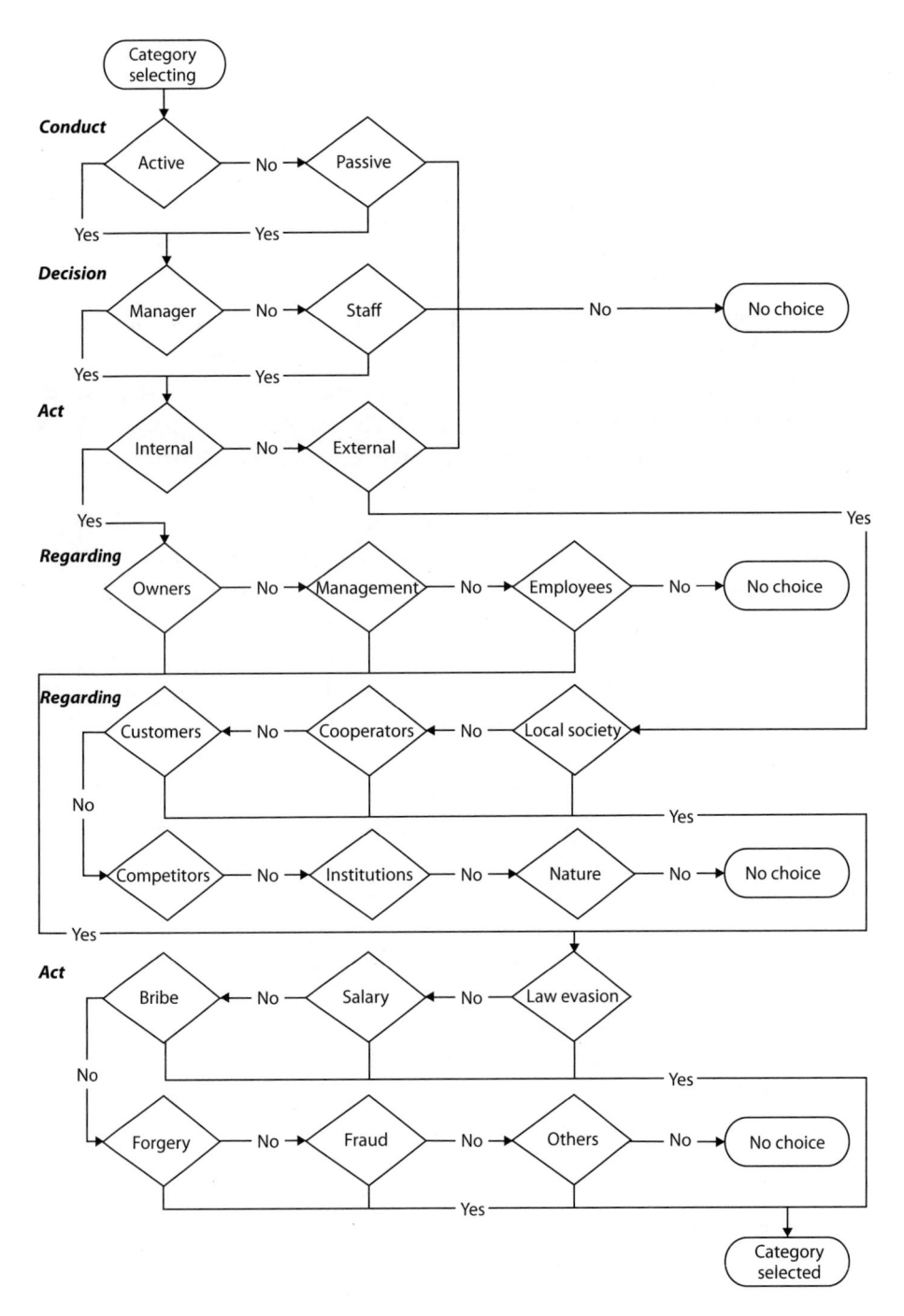

Figure 7.4 Category selecting

Perspectives

Nowadays, computer technology development, particularly the Internet's introduction, creates new possibilities for further evolution of decision support systems; but an expert system that functions by virtue of its information, inferential rules and decision criteria is structurally/functionally/morally/ethically problematic. There clearly emerges significant difficulty in distinguishing between good decisions and good outcomes within the system. Currently available expert systems are a prominent and spectacular, but somewhat confusing example of intersecting ethics and information technology. It seems that even though information technology is still at its infancy, it has already managed to create new figures in ethics – that is, the roles of developers and practitioners of "ethical professionalism". What we refer to are issues that basically extend beyond due diligence on the part of IT professionals during development, even though they may seem to address them only in their professional environment. Ethical DSS serves for purposes of certain changes in personnel, organization structure and process, external competitive pressures, but, most of all, for changes in the decision makers' cognitive strategies of perceiving, classifying and evaluating acts within their environment. They have the potential not only to guide business people through a process of ethical evaluation, but also to fulfil an educational role (Brenner, 2008). However, if rational decisions are to be performed by task-understanding procedures inscribed in computers programs, then how does this affect human rationality and its way of addressing ill-structured decisions? Currently, we dispose of a substantial amount of empirical evidence and studies (which also should be the subject of an in-depth methodological analysis) that human intuitive judgement and decision making can be far from "optimal" in terms of efficiency, and that human judgement abilities deteriorate even further with complexity and stress. Machines are capable of rational formulation, analysing large volumes of information, inductive analysis and, most of all, drawing slow conclusions. They choose optimization strategies based on all possible solutions. People, on the other hand, tend to behave adaptively (because they are "social"); usually have limited access to information; use a more intuitive-deductive search for patterns; rapidly express their personal perceptions; and choose satisfying strategies based on "acceptable" possibilities from the limited range they perceive. What emerges out of this short comparison is a sort of "new ethics" which is, as Hans Moravec (2004) would put it, intrinsically "transhumanist".

In this system, which is not adequate to any moral code of conduct that we elaborated without the assistance of machines, such systems as DSS will actually reflect more closely real-world processes because they will possess the ability of assigning degrees of confidence to various possible options which must be based on the value or variable submitted to measuring, spotting obstacles to group dynamics and predicting communication responses.

Obviously enough, these claims are not new at all. Scientism in the field of ethics has a long-established, although silent tradition. As William H. Whyte (1956) reminds us, the idea of extending mathematics to the affairs of man was very appealing to Descartes, and Thomas Hobbes worked out a complete set of algebraic equations to explain ethics. In 1725 Francis Hutchinson devised an even more elaborate mathematical calculation on morality (Whyte, 1956: 25). The promise was that "with the same techniques that have worked in the physical sciences we can eventually create an exact science of man" (Whyte, 1956: 23). In Chapter 8, "Business Influence on Education", Whyte discusses the part business plays in educational changes:

> *Simply by virtue of the changing economics of university financing, the organization man is going to be much more than an alumnus. As overseer of the corporation's fund giving, he is becoming a sort of extra trustee of education. [...] Give us well-rounded man, business leaders are saying to the colleges, the man steeped in fundamentals; we will give him the specialized knowledge he needs. [...] Convention after convention they make this plea – and their own recruiters go right on doing what they've been doing: demanding more specialists. (Whyte, 1956: 101)*

Now, this generation of bureaucrats is already far in the past, even though it is a past intermingled with the future – a past that is a potentiality of the present. Currently, it is not only about special training, past experience, performance, potential positions and appraisal periods. What we are dealing with is a "hyper-real" version of professionalization and a "hyper-real" version of techniques of recruitment, training, testing and correction, embedded in self-referential virtuality of possibilities. We are not only managing knowledge by means of quantifying, counting and measuring; we are also managing the cognitive dimension of our knowledge: beliefs, ideals, values, schemata and mental models. What we want to share with our computer is not only the joint enterprise but also mutual engagement and the shared repertoire of values, because we believe that together with our machines (animals too, but they do not wish to cooperate on that level) as an organization we will do better.

Thus, ethics transforms itself into a strategic tool that provides crucial information to its "users" and empowers them to make vital decisions. We want computers to correct us, but at the same time we want to connect with them spiritually. We want them and us to be a team.

References

Borzestowski, M. and Waszczyk, M. 2005. Moral Knowledge Expert System: On the borderline between business ethics and new technologies. *Foundations of Control and Management Sciences*, no. 3. Poznan: Poznan University of Technology.

Brenner, B. 2008. A computerised business ethics expert system: A new approach to improving the ethical quality of business decision-making. *Journal of Systemics, Cybernetics and Informatics*, vol. 3, no. 3, 86–90.

Cordeschi, R. 2008. Steps toward the synthetic method: Symbolic information processing and self-organizing systems in early artificial intelligence modeling. In P. Husbands, O. Holland and M. Wheeler (eds), *The Mechanical Mind in History*. Cambridge, MA: MIT Press.

Crosson, F.J. and Sayre, K. (eds) 1967. *Philosophy and Cybernetics: Essays Delivered to the Philosophic Institute for Artificial Intelligence at the University of Notre Dame*. Notre Dame, IN: University of Notre Dame Press.

Dean, C. 2008. A soldier taking orders from its ethical judgment center. *New York Times*, 25 November.

Dreyfus, H.L. 1997. *What Computers Still Can't Do: A Critique of Artificial Reason*. Cambridge, MA: MIT Press.

Dennett, D.C. 1986. Information, technology, and the virtues of ignorance. *Daedalus*, vol. 115, no. 3, 135–53.

Druzdzel, M.J. and Flynn, R.R. 2002. Decision Support Systems. In M.A. Drake (ed.), *Encyclopedia of Library and Information Science*, vol. 1. New York: Marcel Dekker.

Furlong, D. and Vernon, D. 1992. *Reality Paradigms, Perception, and Natural Science: The Relevance of Autopoiesis*. ESPRIT Workshop on Autopoiesis and Perception, Dublin (Dublin City University).

Gilbert, N. and Doran, J. 1994. *Simulating Societies: The Computer Simulation of Social Phenomena*. London: University College London Press.

Halpern, O. 2005. Dreams for our perceptual present: Temporality, storage, and interactivity in cybernetics. *Configurations*, vol. 13, no. 2, 283–319.

Hayward, J. and Varela, F.J. (eds) 1992. *Gentle Bridges: Conversations with the Dalai Lama on the Sciences of Mind*. Boston, MA: Shambhala.

Holland, O. 1997. *Artificial Life*. Cambridge, MA: MIT Press.

Johnson, M. 1987. *The Body in the Mind: The Bodily Basis of Meaning, Imagination, and Reason*. Chicago, IL: University of Chicago Press.

Khalil, O.E.M. 1993. Artificial decision-making and artificial ethics: A management concern. *Journal of Business Ethics*, no. 12, 313–21.

Langacker, R.W. et al. 1995. *Wykłady z gramatyki kognitywnej*. Lublin: Wydawnictwo Uniwersytetu im. Marii Curie-Skłodowskiej.

Latour, B. 1999. *Pandora's Hope: Essays on the Reality of Science Studies*. Cambridge, MA: Harvard University Press.

McKay, D.M. 1956. Towards an information-flow model of human behavior. *British Journal of Psychology*, no. 47, 30–43.

Mirowski, P. 1999. Cyborg Agonistes: Economics meets operations research in mid-century. *Social Studies of Science*, vol. 29, no. 5, 685–718.

Mirowski, P. 2002. *Machine Dreams: Economics Becomes a Cyborg Science*. Cambridge: Cambridge University Press.

Moore, G.E. 1966. *Ethics*, London: Oxford University Press.

Moravec, H. 2004. *Robot Predictions Evolution*. Available at: http://www.frc.ri.cmu.edu/~hpm/project.archive/robot.papers/2004/Predictions.html [accessed 22 May 2014].

Pickering, A. 1995. Cyborg history and the WWII regime. *Perspectives in Science*, no. 3, 1–45.

Simon, H.A. 1986. Decision making and problem solving. *Research Briefings 1986: Report of the Research Briefing Panel on Decision Making and Problem Solving*. Washington, DC: National Academy of Sciences.

Whyte, W.H. 1956. *The Organization Man*. New York: Simon and Shuster.

Chapter 8

Qualitative Research on the Organization of Work in Internet Prosumer Projects

SEBASTIAN SKOLIK

Introduction

There are two essential issues which a researcher has to cope with while getting ready to research: which research methods he will use and whether intends to discover new phenomena and processes or present them as universal ones with regard to current knowledge. New fields of research, such as cyberspace, induce searching what is exotic and unique. Frequently, it may lead to creating artefacts and the inflation of terms and concepts. However, regardless of the researcher's attitude, he has to determine which methods he will use in order to describe and explain discovered phenomena. In case of research on large prosumer communities such as Wikimedia[1] quantitative methods may appear more attractive. Prosumer communities include those in which individuals create products or content of symbolic culture and in which the division into producers and consumers is blurred (Tapscott and Williams, 2008). What is special in the case of Wikimedia is that they gather non-professional knowledge workers who process and share knowledge among themselves and make it available to the rest of the Internet users. Thanks to their activity the knowledge becomes a common good (Hofmokl, 2009).

Creating and analysing the database of these projects leads to building multiple indicators, which enables us to compare the quality of the produced content, the effectiveness of activities, to shape the social structure and many

---

[1] Wikimedia projects are described as the websites for which the Wikimedia Foundation is legally and technically responsible: Wikipedia in several hundred language versions and its sister projects.

others. Nevertheless, in case of researchers who do not know the specificity of functioning of those communities, as well as people who are participants focused on quantitative analysis, the results of the research may be shallow (Jemielniak, 2013: 276–7). Even if the researchers interpret the result of the analysis through their reference to the intersubjective experience, in the case of comparative studies – e.g. comparing trends between language versions of Wikipedia – they are not able to distinguish the differences in organizational culture of these projects. Qualitative research allow us to define particular situations which lead to specific activities (Silverman, 2009: 28) and to track the processes resulting in the creation of given phenomena – e.g. rituals or forms of institutionalization.

The division into qualitative and quantitative research is not always sharp (Silverman, 2008: 32; Kozinets, 2012: 68). With regard to the content analysis one can use the statistical tools helping to search terms or phrases (even in the contextual form) essential from the point of view of the research problem (Bendkowski, 2012). In order to achieve the desired result in qualitative research one should use multiple methods and, if possible, multiple tools, not avoiding at the same time the secondary analysis of the data collected in the quantitative research. What is essential in a qualitative study is exploring the problem, the cognition of subjective experience of the researched reality. This, however, requires presence in the collectivity, and therefore connects with the question of the influence of the researcher on the studied phenomenon. Nevertheless, also in the survey research the researcher influences the reality through the choice of particular questions in a questionnaire. Frequently, the participants of the social life have not asked themselves these questions, or these questions have not been significant for them at all in the context of a given social problem. From the netnographic perspective, which is the expansion of the ethnographic approach, analysis of the empirical material is based on two kinds of data: not induced (naturally occurring data) and induced (manufactured data) by the researcher (Kozinets, 2012: 152–68). In the first case the researcher does not interfere in the reality, but it is possible that he will not get the answers to the research questions essential for him. When a researcher immerses himself in the activity in a given collectivity, it may paradoxically result in getting awareness of what the effect of his interference is. However, he may lose the objectivity. All in all, what is important is that the qualitative research focuses on particular cases, which are more "accidental". They are connected with the idiographic perspective (emic), not the nomothetic one (etic) (Denzin and Lincoln, 2009: 36).

The choice of the research strategy is connected with the research problem. In cases of the study of the work organization it is important to answer the following questions. What are the forms of the work organization? How do the workgroups come into existence? How are the responsibilities delegated? How do the processes of reaching consensus run? How do the hierarchy forms? How do the processes of recruitment and selection run? These questions may seem trivial; however, they are not so with reference to the prosumer communities. Since creating the content (the product) is based on the volunteer work, which is not formalized, there is no problem with the ownership, remuneration and, in consequence, the economic constraint. Additionally, due to the fact that the anonymity of the users is largely an appreciated value, the problem of identity occurs. However, as in the case of other web collectivities (Castells, 2003: 137), the majority of active participants do not change their own identity.

The Researcher Enters the Virtual Theatre Stage

An important issue in the classic field research is the possibility of conducting the study inside the collectivity. It is possible through taking an appropriate role (Agar, 1980) which persuades the collectivity to accept the presence of the researcher or by finding the "porter" (Hammersley and Atkinson, 2001). In netnographic research, especially in the qualitative research of egalitarian collectivities, entering the field seems quite simple. In the case of Wikimedia, some of the most dynamic prosumer projects, the researcher has to create an account (however, he can participate even without it) and learn the rules of activity. What is important here is the recognition of the unwritten rules and the attitude of the individuals towards them. A part of the rules is codified and another part is set in the course of discussion, yet is not easily accessible. Codified rules are presented to newcomers right at the beginning or after some time (it is different depending on the language version or sister project of Wikipedia). They are available in the corresponding bookmarks (which were hidden until 2010, when a new interface appeared) of the side menu: "Help", "Community portal", "Policies and guidelines". They refer to the rules of creating the content as well as to the principles of netiquette. The interpretation of detailed regulations is not explicit and learning them all is often impossible without previous attempts at active activity.

The researcher who has not been an editor before initially has an opportunity to experience at least some of the ways in which newcomers are treated. This is one of the most significant problems among wikipedists (Jemielniak, 2013: 125), whose number is decreasing with the years (Skolik, 2013). Kozinets defined these kinds of prosumer collectivities as "the communities of maniacs", juxtaposing them with "the communities of builders", which were by contrast described as more involved in creating the social relations (Kozinets, 2012: 60).[2] The collectivities oriented on common creation of content attach less significance to those relations because they are focused on performing specific tasks – creating the entries in the encyclopedia or other articles, depending on the project. An individual who is initially focused on the interactions, not on editing the articles, may even be subject to oppression by other users. Therefore it is crucial for a researcher not to start from a discussion unless it is a discussion with reference to the substantive content. However, in some Wikipedias the researches on the projects have been institutionalized and the rules of cooperation between the collectivity and the scientific environment have been set.[3] Issuing an appeal to the collectivity does not necessarily mean that one will accept conducting the research on oneself. Nevertheless, the institutional "porter" exists for this situation.

In the title of this subsection "the stage" is mentioned, but the main problem is the identification of the backstage. All activities on Wikipedia are recorded. In the case of gaining appropriate entitlements (of "the administrator") a user can get access to deleted content as well. Focusing only on the records of the web pages of the project does not allow us to go backstage, even if a researcher makes notes while observing their creation on an ongoing basis. Although the terms "stage" and "backstage" are relative because there is also a show behind the scenes yet for a smaller audience (Goffman, 2000), their identification enables us to study specific activities of the users. It particularly concerns the activities influencing the functioning of the whole project or collectivity. One of the most significant issues is finding the communication channels which generate messages not available to the public. Using instant messengers, electronic mail or chats enables an individual to comment backstage on reality and to transpose the meaning (keying). If certain forms of interaction are available to the public, they can have the form of fun or a joke behind the scenes (Goffman, 2010: 37–40); or, on the other hand, they can be explained more comprehensibly backstage. Sometimes, so as not to escalate the conflicts, the

---

[2] In the article the term "collectivity" is used with reference to the editors of the Wikipedia, because not all language versions have got so many users to be able to describe them as a community. In small projects it is even possible for the significant relationships between the users not to exist. Some of them consist of a few or several active editors. On the following web page the number of editors active in a given language version during the last month is listed. See http://s23.org/wikistats/wikipedias_html.php?sort=ausers_asc [accessed 20 May 2014]. The tool that serves for acquiring the data is not precise. Yet, it is possible to verify the activity of an editor by visiting the register of recent changes in the projects. The same problem is visible in other prosumer environments.

[3] See http://en.wikipedia.org/wiki/Wikipedia:What_are_these_researchers_doing_in_my_Wikipedia%3F; http://en.wikipedia.org/wiki/Wikipedia:Don%27t_bite_the_researchers.

fabrications may be translated. The fabrications are described by Goffman as a form of deceit, far-reaching manipulation of impressions (Goffman, 2010: 67–8). In Internet jargon a part of the most sophisticated fabrication is called trolling (Kamińska, 2008). One should be aware of the additional communication channels of an open (public) character – public mailing lists, "official" Internet Relay Chat (IRC) channels, Facebook profiles.

Participant and Non-Participant Observation

The participant observation method is one of the crucial methods in qualitative research. It differs from the non-participant one in that the researcher takes a role in a particular collectivity and is able to learn the functioning of the role-playing system and especially to recognize the aspects of the role which he takes in the collectivity (Mayntz et al., 1985: 126–9). Taking a role or several roles[4] allows us to determine the meaning of a given role in a self-reflective and intersubjective way (Jemielniak, 2013). What is typical for the participant observation is that switching the roles of the researcher and the participant is quite dubious. In order to avoid the dissonance, it is preferable to use the secret participant observation, especially with regard to the discovering of behind-the-scenes activity. The problem of participation is connected with a question of identity. As regards the web pages based on the wiki software, in most cases the presence of a user is visible only while performing an activity, specifically during the recording of the edited articles. The case is different when using Internet chats or some of the Internet forums where "logging in" means admitting to "being here". However, a non-active individual need not necessarily be outside those places. Not admitting to the fact of conducting the survey is tantamount to hiding the identity. Taking and testing numerous roles allows someone to appear under different pseudonyms. Yet, this kind of manipulation impedes the observation of a spontaneous process of role changes, rites of passage and similar events.

It is not possible to take all roles; but for a thorough knowledge of social reality, taking a lot of them gives better opportunities to analyse the acting of a given role by others. It concerns to a great extent behaviour such as making decisions, expressing opinions, using sanctions or leading workgroups. Taking into consideration the egalitarian character of the prosumer projects, achieving the positions which allow one to play these roles is not so difficult. In many

---

4 In the egalitarian collectivities there is no formal organizational structure which would impose positions and roles; therefore it is easier and more frequent to take social roles.

cases, the participants of such collectivities expect others to take specific roles so that they themselves could focus on performing substantive work. Since the actual participation manifests in action, the participant observation is not sufficient in the areas where the researcher has not enough competence – e.g. in cases of analyzing workgroups editing the issues of mathematics or medicine on Wikipedia when they have not got the knowledge in this respect.

It is reasonable at this stage to accept the following research strategies:

1. Non-participant observation is chosen when a researcher has not got proper competence to take a particular role – e.g. in the case of learning codified axio-normative system before starting the activity as a newbie. It may also take the form of making observations of the way in which the collectivity treats newbies.

2. Participant observation is chosen when a researcher gets appropriate competence to accept a given role. It may be, e.g., the role of a leader of a "subproject"[5] or an administrator on the web page Wikinews, providing civic Internet journalism.

3. Non-participant observation is once more used by a researcher with regard to other participants playing a given role at the moment of leaving this role by a researcher.

As it has been already emphasized, what is characteristic for an online collectivity is the fact that the presence of a participant is not always visible. Taking part in particular activities intertwines with the non-participant observation of the activity of others. It may concern observing different indications of activities, mutual interactions, commenting or observing the changes of particular pages. Editing the content of entries on Wikipedia is not the most eminent example of communication action, yet it may be perceived in that way. It may be a transposition of the discussion with other users in which a researcher has previously been involved. Recognizing substantial roles and the significant others who influence the functioning of particular fields of projects may also allow a researcher to abandon the participant observation. Abandoning it may happen when the roles taken by a researcher influence too much the social life which is being observed. However, the complete withdrawal from participation

---

5 So-called WikiProjects have been functioning for a few years within Wikimedia. They are internal projects on certain subjects or fields of activity, such as WikiProjects concerning psychology or focusing on specific technical activities.

may result in a researcher's inability to learn new, crucial events influencing the work organization. A new event may be exemplified by a technological change, such as introducing the notification system on Wikipedia.[6] One of the results of this mechanism is that users can thank each other for performing given editions and this information is not recorded on the project's website. In this case a researcher may decide to create a new identity owing to which he will not be involved in former activity.

Field Experiments in a Bazaar Environment

As opposed to professional organizations, prosumers act in environments with no formalized structure, whether they are hackers creating free software or wikipedists. This facilitates accepting a bazaar way of creating the content. It basically means that there is no plan of action imposed from above, there is no established division of labour and the content is created through continuous changing (Raymond 1999). Paradoxically, the effects of this are the products that are equal to the professional ones, which often depend on the number of the prosumers who create them. Hence, it is still experimenting, also in terms of work organization.

In classic organizations a planned action is described with a number of norms and the researcher may search for the dissents, shaping the informal structures, emerging specific, not revealed elements of an organizational culture (Hofstede, 2007). Accepting the classification of R.K. Merton (2002: 205–17), one can tell that the dominant deviation in the classic organization is ritualism; and innovations, from the point of view of the possible benefits for an organization, seem very rarely occurring "goods". The attitude of a researcher may lead to excessive focus on searching new forms of activity, and as a consequence to losing sight of deeper processes occurring in the researched collectivities. In the prosumer environment the actions are the result of the individual motivations and are ruled by flexible guidelines, not rigid standards (Kulesza, 2010: 52–6). What can be more attractive research problems here are the processes of institutionalization and hierarchy, which are the phenomena that the researched collectivities are less conscious of. In order to immerse themselves in the life of a collectivity a researcher should rather accept an attitude of an innovator rather than of an individual ritually performing actions. The innovators making or proposing changes have more

---

6   The description of the functioning of this tool is available at http://en.wikipedia.org/wiki/Wikipedia:Notifications [accessed 20 May 2014].

possibilities to go backstage. Even if the propositions of changes are not accepted, they are always welcome.

This results in long-range consequences in terms of active participation of a researcher. First of all he influences the researched reality far more often than in other kinds of study. The more significant the role for a collectivity, the more interference occurs. Although the actions of the other "significant others" may be treated as natural experiments (Babbie, 2003: 263), it is important to realize that in certain circumstances a participant observation changes into a field experiment. In this kind of experiment the complete control of the conditions is not possible, yet the researcher can control the manipulation of variables while creating the experimental situation (Nachmias and Nachmias, 2001: 235–6). Conducting the experimental research, whether it is a natural experiment or a controlled one, is a step towards quantitative research, for what is important here is the measurement. However, rejecting this perspective does not seem sensible, even while conducting qualitative research.

Here comes the question if the exaggerated controlling of own actions may lead to excluding one's own natural commitment which is required for proper interpretation of the occurring processes. It seems that it is a dilemma quite difficult to solve. Involvement in the prosumer environment leads inevitably to the negotiation of performing particular tasks. If it is natural, with time, one can spontaneously take a role of an expert sharing the knowledge of work organization during the negotiations. The leadership roles, however – and not only them – are connected with expert power in this kind of environment (Wallace, 2003: 136–8). Despite the fact that the prosumers are focused on creating the content, the discussions held on the meta-level usually concern the issues regarding creating rules and work organization procedures. When a researcher does not control his own involvement, he may take unique roles which are the artefacts with regard to the researched social structure. By means of his own actions he can catalyse the processes which in other circumstances would not have appeared or induce phenomena of the nature of artefacts. Hence, most beneficial seems to be treating one's own actions as natural experiments and analysing their results ex post, not excluding the quantitative measurement.

Netnographic Interviews and Creating Focus Groups

One of the effects of involvement in the social life of prosumers is greater trust from the prosumers when at some moment a user reveals himself as a professional researcher. It may happen when he wants to carry out research by means of interview, whether standarised interview or not.

Otherwise, when the independent subjects ask for an interview, the participants may object. It is noticeable in the case of Wikipedia, where a significant number of wikipedists are scientists in private and it is they who make accusations. As examples may serve two situations which have occurred on the mailing list of the Polish Wikipedia.

One of the following situations happened in July 2011. A committed wikipedist placed on the mailing list a request for participation in research organized by researchers from the Polish–Japanese Institute of Information Technology:

Mag[7]

The Wikiteams scientific research has just started. It concerns the phenomena of creating the workteams in Wikipedia and their influence on the shaping the substantive content of the project. Many of you may remember the authors of the research related to PJWSTK from our conferences and rallies, including Wikimania. They have prepared to the research very thoroughly and the results of their inquiries look promising so I think that it is worth helping them by filling in the questionnaire.

After half an hour a response to the message occurred. Another committed Wikipedia user discouraged people from participating in the research due to not abiding by the procedures.

Chemik

As I have already written on Facebook, I don't like this research. There is no information about the names of the scientists who conduct it, there is lack of any contact details to organizers, it is not known within what kind of scientific program the research is conducted, there is no information about the privacy policy (ensuring about the anonymity is not enough). There is no reliable description of the aims of the research. The research has not been reported on a proper meta-page.

---

7   Instead of names/pseudonyms cryptonyms have been used. However, the course of the cited statements is available to the public on the archival pages of the mailing list. Available at: http://lists.wikimedia.org/pipermail/wikipl-l [accessed 20 May 2014]. The cryptonyms of the wikipedists are in bold.

> http://meta.wikimedia.org/wiki/Research/Projects
>
> *Are the results of the research going to be available under a free licence? I advise you against participating in this research because it is contradictory to the general recommendations for these kind of research prepared by the following:*
>
> http://meta.wikimedia.org/wiki/Research_Policy
>
> http://meta.wikimedia.org/wiki/Notes_on_good_practices_on_Wikipedia_research
>
> *Compiled by the committee for researches of Wikimedia Foundation*

The procedures which were cited by a wikipedist were established in order to indicate potential problems during preparation to conduct a research. In this case the researchers were presented as people who had already done research concerning Polish language speaking collectivity. In a significantly worse situation are the people who have not been recognized among editors yet. One situation like this took place in March 2012. An unknown user appeared on the mailing list, having invited people to participate in a research project on the Wikipedia pages before:

> **MF**
>
> *I want to remind of pending research of the Wikipedists who are professionally active. There has been a weak response up till now. If you work professionally and you are an active Wikipedist this research is just for you. The research questionnaires are sent via e-mail and filling them in takes only several minutes. Completing this research will allow us to widen the knowledge of the special group of people which you, Wikipedists, in my opinion are. The research aims at measuring the level of motivation, the need of own individuality as well as the work ethics. I hope all the time that we will manage to finish this research and if you have some time, please write me an e-mail and I will send you a questionnaire in response. Every person eager to take part in the research is greatly helpful. I will gladly accept all proposals of help to reach more Wikipedists.*

One of the reactions which appeared on the list the next day was above all the enumeration of the weaknesses of the research tool:

BN

The questionnaire is prepared from the perspective of the researcher's needs, not from the perspective of the needs of the respondents, who want to help and devote their time. It is not a simple questionnaire in Word but extended one in Excel placed in several sheets, ugly, with illegible layout, made with minimum effort. If it was my questionnaire, I would CARE about the cooperation with the respondents. That is why I excused myself from the research, despite having agreed to help before. I do not intend to help someone who is lazy. It must be the very low quality of the research which is the reason for classifying the questionnaire.

In both quoted examples of research the questionnaires for the standardized interview have been prepared. In both cases the following ethical problems were implicitly indicated: unspecified privacy policy and lack of adjustment to the needs of the respondents. The second problem is particularly interesting. In a similar way are criticized the survey researches conducted annually by the Wikimedia Foundation, where the majority of questions in the online questionnaire concern the functioning of this organization. The approaches mentioned above may be presented in the *etic* perspective. The researchers impose their issues, while the participants of the collectivity expect the research concerning other issues significant for them. The requests for participation in a research project do not appear in this particular environment very often, which does not result in fatigue with constant "tearing away from work" for the collectivity. However, the lack of compatibility of the researcher's interests with the interests of the users resulted in the boycott of the research (Kozinets, 2012: 114–15).

In the survey research the question of a pollster's influence is raised. The factors which may influence the answers of the respondents are social characteristics of a pollster: among others, easy to identify characteristics such as sex, race or character traits which have been revealed in the course of interaction (Sztabiński, 1997: 145–65). In a digital environment the social characteristics are less visible, yet it may cause the need of their defining by the respondents. Considering the possibility of concealing many of one's own characteristics, one can assume that the strongest influencing factor is perceiving the researcher as a "professional stranger". It may lead to a lack of trust, and hence to the violation of the ontological security (Giddens, 2002: 51–4). It is so significant because trusting others requires definite distancing from the uncertainty of the Internet user's identity. Consequently, obtaining information about views, attitudes or values requires greater commitment in order to gain trust. One can accept the following research strategies:

- conducting individual free interviews in order to gain trust and accustom the collectivity with a researcher;

- conducting the interviews in focus groups if the trust of the key actors is gained;

- conducting the survey research if one is sure of the trust of the significant part of active users and when the interviews among small numbers of people are not sufficient compared to the intended research problems;

- conducting in-depth interviews aimed at better understanding and interpreting the results collected in the survey research or in the previous free interviews.

Using the method of interview allows researchers to understand the structure of the meaning attributed to an observed action (Weber, 2002: 8–9). It is not possible during making observations. Sharing information about personal motivations, views or values is not easy for the interviewed person because of certain emotional costs. An interviewed person usually presents himself in a favourable light (Sztabiński, 1997: 157). What is more, the answers to the questions are the outcome of the intensity of reaction on the side of the researcher and the outcome of the economy of answers on the side of the interviewed person. Many times a respondent searches for the scheme of answers or creates the scheme (Sułek, 2001: 145–8). It also happens in cases of using the standardized interviews which impose the framework of the process of interaction. However, it is difficult to determine, with regard to free interviews, whether the statements are formulated narration or the researcher has got direct access to the experience (Silverman, 2008: 78–9).

What is crucial issue here is not only how to reach the intersubjective social reality but also how to reach the perspective of perceiving this reality, unrevealed to the other actors. It is important to ask oneself a few questions:

- Who should be treated as an expert?

- In what circumstances should the interviews be conducted in order to reach the framework of meanings?

- Which places for possible interviews with the participants of the prosumer collectivity are the most advantageous in terms of obtaining information on the way in which participants perceive themselves?

In cases of interviews conducted in a "natural" environment of the prosumers, it seems that one can get better access to their intersubjective reality. Yet, simultaneously, it is the public not an intimate space. By contrast, when the interaction is confidential – by private messaging (PM) – the statements may take on a character of formulated narration. Oftentimes, fabrications occur. And, finally, what is important is also to what extent the conversation is closer to a natural one: if the interview is made face to face, by means of chats, wiki pages or email correspondence. Every one of the mentioned ways has its limitations. The most advantageous seems to be the synchronous conversation, during which one can experience a mutual presence in a given place. Yet, not every prosumer is available enough so that a researcher is able to conduct a live conversation with them. Moreover, not everyone is eager to use the communication forms not typical for their professional environment. Using many techniques and confronting them may give more insight in the quality of the collected data. Apart from that, it is crucial to take into consideration that the medium is the message (McLuhan, 2001).

What is also important is defining the experts who are going to take part in the interviews. For a newbie an expert may be a person who has proper knowledge and considerable experience in order to "tell the story" about one's own biography and the processes observed by this person. However, if a researcher wants to learn the attitudes of the newbies towards particular problems, he should treat them as experts. People who have just begun to act face a situation in which they have to define the meaning of existing social phenomena by themselves. Between the newbies and the advanced users the whole spectrum of the participants of the collectivity extends. The participants of the collectivity partially accept the rules of functioning and partially dissent from some rules. A part of the participants may use defensive provocations so as to reduce the ambivalence towards the existing axio-normative system and create their own subcultures (Siemaszko, 1993: 143–4). The possibility of conducting free interviews among this part of the collectivity also requires the trust that brings the dilemma on the question of taking the roles by a researcher. Too much support from the conformist participants may ruin the trust of the dissenters. It is probably not possible for one researcher to conduct a research project based on the method of free interview among the conformists and nonconformists with the same result. However, if it is possible for natural experiments to occur, one can take the initiative during the spontaneous discussions. In these spontaneously created focus groups the dissenters are revealed. Yet, their statements should not necessarily be treated as sincere, because they aim at exerting influence in order to gain supporters, especially if the discussion is held in public, not behind the scenes.

Due to the fact that the discussions concern problems significant to the prosumers, directing the discussions also to the subjects crucial for the research requires a certain sense of time of work. One can observe in a 24-hour cycle that the discussions are more intensive in the evening hours when the prosumers are not occupied with their duties connected with their functioning in "real life". Hence, it is a question of the time when one can tear the prosumers away from their work. On the other hand, bringing up the "important subjects" during the holidays may be questioned because they should be brought up when larger numbers of users would be able to take part in a debate. An important factor is also the time that has passed since the last discussion on a similar subject. However, in some cases when the subject matter returns one can initiate creating a special focus group. It may take place over the Internet or sometimes a heated dispute may lead to conducting the "workshop" offline. Large collectivities of prosumers quite often initiate face-to-face meetings in order to discuss particular problems connected with the organization of work. Being a member of an egalitarian collectivity allows one in a natural way to take part in the meetings as well as to lead the discussions. Behind the scenes, "natural" focus groups may be also be led by nonconformist subcultures. Taking part in them would require resignation from the role of a professional expert among the conformists or generating a new identity.

The last issue worth mentioning is the question of making the results of the research available. If the collected data do not allow one to get an insight into the researched problem, the members of the prosumer collectivities may spontaneously express their criticism of the results of the research. With regard to the research on the wikipedists, such critical opinions occur very often. Moreover, the experts who have not taken part in the research before reveal themselves. These situations overcome the resistance that might have occurred in the previous conversations and facilitate the conducting of the in-depth interviews. It might be an opportunity to initiate the creation of focus groups and consequently to get more detailed data.

Notes from the Field and Archive Data

Collecting data from Internet prosumer projects generally does not differ from ways of collecting data in netnography. However, an activity such as prosumption is specific in terms of the ways of creating the content. If a given file, whether it is a text file or graphic file,[8] may be changed several times, the research should focus not only on what is visible to the receiver but also on the history of the data. What is also specific is that the knowledge and the software are permanently processed and that access to these operations is open. Since these changes occur at different times access only to the archival data may not be sufficient. Current observation of the activity of the prosumer collectivity allows one to find a context to the modifications. In case of the data available before the beginning of the observation or during the observer's absence, the observer may search the context of the events on other pages, crucial for the project pages. He may also question in conversation the users active at that time about the needed context.

On account of the issues mentioned above, there is a need for making notes from the field. Apart from the comments, it is advisable to add to the results of the observation the screenshots if the interface of the project changes often and links to previously observed pages or particular versions of the pages. If one analyses the deleted content of the project, copies of the deleted content should also be collected provided that one has been granted the access to these kinds of files. When a large amount of data is collected there is a need for their systematic categorization (Kozinets, 2012: 153–8). Last but not least important is determining the place where the data will be stored. Since the process of collecting is carried on simultaneously with the current analysis (Silverman, 2008: 95), the most appropriate for this purpose seems to be a private notebook. If the initial analysis is not going to influence the research problems by changing them, one may involve the users, who in this case should be treated as experts. Such place may be, e.g., the page of a user in the researched Wikimedia project. A considerable number of wikipedists make their own notes from observations of the functioning of the project, and some of the wikipedists place the results of their research in scientific publications.[9] Moreover, for the short-term collection of data one can use the bookmark system of the browser, an email archive folder and, if the research is conducted in teams, also a service page for storing data, such as Dropbox. Text files containing the analysis may be a part of this archiving system. Even if the files collected in this way are not analysed instantly due to time factors, they can be treated as reminders.

---

8   As regards the web pages based on the Wiki software and its mutations, every page is an editable file.
9   A large yet not complete base of articles on wiki pages is available on the WikiPapers page. Available at: http://wikipapers.referata.com/wiki/Main_Page [accessed 20 May 2014]. Some of them are available in open access mode and some are published under a free licence.

With regard to the research of the work organization in Wikimedia projects, both the editable pages and the registers can be treated as the archive data. In the case of the latter, a considerable number of them are available only at a given time. Hence, if they are taken into consideration, their copies should be created as well. These are, for example, the lists of the users who have particular entitlements in a given time, the registers of the operations on the files or the registers of administrative activity. As regards the editable web pages of the projects, one may categorize them as follows.

- The user pages and their subpages where they can make personal notes and define their own identity, personal views and values as well as the visions of the development of the project and its criticism.

- The user discussion pages where one may find comments on a given user's activity, requests for help, requests for consultations, agitations for participation in a given undertaking in the project.

- So-called meta-pages,[10] among which one can distinguish the pages serving as a general discussion forum; pages dedicated to concrete, narrow undertakings; pages serving as a notice board; pages dedicated to submitting requests; pages dedicated to the evaluation of the quality of passwords; and finally the pages where debates on granting and taking away the entitlements of particular users take place. These kinds of page may be categorized by using the internal categorization mechanism.

The generated statistical data set may be treated as a specific type of archival data. A considerable part of them is placed in both projects and in publications. In this respect the polemics of the projects often flow between the users and the researcher's environment. The field of research may also be the process of negotiating the usability of the indicators which determine: the quality of the content; the commitment of the users; the openness to the newbies; the level of automation of activity and so on.[11] Since quantitative data may be useful in qualitative research to outline the scale of the phenomenon, in the case of lack of competence to process the database dump, one can get help from the

---

10 Depending on the language versions, these are the pages starting with prefixes (Wikipedia, WikiProject), Help and the discussion pages related to them.
11 The sets of statistical data and their description are available on the English-language Wikipedia and its equivalents in different language versions. See https://en.wikipedia.org/wiki/Wikipedia:Statistics [accessed 20 May 2014].

other prosumers. The usefulness of the data depends on how precisely the methodology of collecting and generating the data has been defined. In the case of statistical data obtained from processing the databases, a substantial part of them is based on estimates – e.g. the number of editing users or the number of visits to web pages. The statistics showing the increase in the number of passwords, prepared by the Dutch wikipedist Erik Zachte, may serve as an example.[12] His set does not include the articles which were deleted later. If the same methodology is used with respect to the number of users, the data probably does not take into account the users who have edited only the deleted articles. Observing the changes in this kind of summary allows one to define the degree of their precision in order to use them for interpretation of the course of the processes.

Final Remarks

Recognizing the phenomena and processes occurring in prosumer environments may depend on the position of the researcher towards prosumption. It would be safe to assume that initially a researcher's own attitude towards this new way of creating content is not neutral. Identifying one's own position towards the object of research allows one to determine the level of its neutrality. It may have an effect on the process of obtaining competence in the researched environment and on the easiness of taking roles and the degree of commitment. Furthermore, it may influence one's own reactions to criticism of the researched project, especially criticism from the academic environment. On the one hand the internalization of the prosumer values may facilitate learning the reality in which the boundary between consumption and production is blurred. On the other hand it may cause some difficulties with translating the perspective of a participant into the perspective of a researcher describing a phenomenon, especially if his environment is far from these values.

One can say that if a given field of human activity is subjected to research, it means that one is interested in the environment and its values. The environments discussed in the chapter may be attractive not only due to the cognitive reason but also because they allow one to develop one's creativity. Frequent and long spending time in them may change the perception of the social (and other) reality to a considerable degree. The committed users of Wikimedia spend their time on projects for even several hours a day with a few week-long breaks per year. Switching the roles of an amateur participant

---

12 See http://stats.wikimedia.org/EN/TablesArticlesTotal.htm [accessed 20 May 2014].

and a professional researcher requires additional time for the reduction of stress. Immersing oneself in the research of prosumer collectivity may require a change of lifestyle, especially a change of organization of one's personal and professional life.

Summary

This chapter is a presentation of the methods of qualitative research with reference to Internet prosumer environments. Prosumption, being the combination of consumer activity and the common creating the content, may be treated as a specific field of research on the organization of work. This phenomenon began to gain in strength in the first decade of the twenty-first century, yet the analysis of the prosumer collectivities was based on quantitative research. By contrast, the qualitative methods, including the netnographic ones, often focused on the areas in which the problems connected with the work organization were of less importance. Since Wikimedia projects are unique places on the Internet, which gather unprofessional knowledge workers, a considerable part of the chapter was dedicated to the research of these projects.

The described research strategies relate to the ways of collecting the existing (naturally occurring) data and the induced (manufactured) data as well as to the problem of the involvement of a researcher in the life of the researched collectivities. The problems connected with using the following methods: observations (participant and non-participant), interviews, focus groups and field experiments have been specified.

Key words: prosumption, work organization, qualitative research, virtual collectivities.

References

Agar, M. (1980). *The Professional Stranger: An Informal Introduction to Ethnography*. New York: Academic Press.
Babbie, E. (2003). *Badania społeczne w praktyce*. Warsaw: PWN.
Bendkowski, J. (2012). Zachowania komunikacyjne głównych aktorów wirtualnych sieci wiedzy. *Menagement*, 16(1), 624–36.
Castells, M. (2003). *Galaktyka Internetu. Refleksje nad Internetem, biznesem i społeczeństwem*. Poznań: Rebis.

Denzin, N.K. and Lincoln, Y.S. (eds) (2009). *Metody badań jakościowych*. Warsaw: PWN.
Gidddens, A. (2002). *Nowoczesność i tożsamość. "Ja" i społecześntwo w epoce późnej nowoczesności*. Warsaw: PWN.
Goffman, E. (2000). *Człowiek w teatrze życia codziennego*. Warsaw: Wydawnictwo KR.
Goffman, E. (2010). *Analiza ramowa*. Krakow: Zakład Wydawniczy NOMOS.
Hammersley, M. and Atkinson, P. (2001). *Metody badań terenowych*. Poznań: Zysk i S-ka.
Hofmokl, J. (2009). *Internet jako nowe dobro wspólne*. Warsaw: Wydawnictwa Akademickie i Profesjonalne.
Hofstede, G. (2007). *Kultury i organizacje*. Warsaw: PWE.
Jemielniak, D. (2013). *Życie wirtualnych dzikich. Netnografia Wikipedii, najwiekszego projektu współtworzonego przez ludzi*. Warsaw: Poltex.
Kamińska, M. (2008). Flaming i trolling. Kulturotwórcza rola konfliktu we wspólnocie wirtualnej. In M. Wawrzak-Chodaczek (ed.), *Komunikacja społeczna w świecie wirtualnym*. Toruń: Wydawnictwo Adam Marszałek, 280–96.
Kozinets, R.V. (2012). *Netnografia: Badania etnograficzne online*. Warsaw: PWN.
Kulesza, J. (2010). *Ius internet. Między prawem a etyką*. Warsaw: Wydawnictwa Akademickie i Profesjonalne.
Mayntz, R., Holm, K. and Hübner, P. (1985). *Wprowadzenie do metod socjologii empirycznej*. Warsaw: PWN.
Merton, R.K. (2002). *Teoria socjologiczna i struktura społeczna*. Warsaw: PWN.
McLuhan, M. (2001). *Understanding Media: The Extensions of Man*. London: Routledge.
Nachmias, Ch. F. and Nachmias, D. (2001). *Metody badawcze w naukach społecznych*. Poznań: Zysk i S-ka.
Raymond, E. (1999). The cathedral and the bazaar. *Knowledge, Technology and Policy*, 12(3), 23–49.
Siemaszko, A. (1993). *Granice tolerancji. O teoriach zachowań dewiacyjnych*. Warsaw: PWN.
Silverman, D. (2008). *Prowadzenie badań jakościowych*. Warsaw: PWN.
Silverman, D. (2009). *Interpretacja danych jakościowych*. Warsaw: PWN.
Skolik, S. (2013). Migracje użytkowników w przestrzeni Internetu. In D. Jelonek and T. Turek (eds), *Wiedza i technologie informacyjne. Nowe trendy badań i aplikacji*. Częstochowa: SWWZ PCz, 168–78.
Sułek, A. (2001). *Sondaż polski*. Warsaw: Wydawnictwo IFiS PAN.
Sztabiński, P.B. (1997). *Ankieterzy i ich respondenci. Od kogo zależą wyniki badań ankietowych*. Warsaw: Wydawnictwo IFiS PAN.
Tapscott, D. and Williams, A.D. (2008). *Wikinomia. O globalnej współpracy, która zmienia wszystko*. Warsaw: Wydawnictwa Akademickie i Profesjonalne.

Wallace, P. (2003). *Psychologia Internetu*. Poznań: Rebis.
Weber, M. (2002). *Gospodarka i społeczeństwo. Zarys socjologii rozumiejącej*. Warsaw: PWN.

Chapter 9

Innovative Networks in Knowledge-Intensive Industries: How to Make Them Work? An Empirical Investigation into the Polish Aviation Valley

WOJCIECH CZAKON and PATRYCJA KLIMAS

Since the seminal study on biotechnology's networked innovation (Powell et al., 1996) a growing research interest has been allocated to the environment where knowledge is being explored, generated and then exploited. Networks increasingly come into focus, as they are oriented on innovations acquiring (Capaldo, 2007) and perceived as a source of innovation themselves (Kogut, 2000). We adopt the view of an innovation network as a set of organizations and relationships between them, oriented at information acquisition, knowledge access and sharing, continuous learning, R&D activities and knowledge commercialization (Dhanaraj and Parkhe, 2006). We believe that innovation networks provide a framework for examining knowledge-intensive industries.

Beyond the mere recognition of collaborative knowledge generation (Haagedorn, 1993), until recently very few studies focused on the roles played by actors in innovative networks (Czakon and Klimas, 2011). Prior literature states that such networks are asymmetric and that the engagement of various actors differs significantly. We argue that some network nodes play distinctive roles and take responsibility for the processes of network leadership. In the literature, the network leadership has been scrutinized under different labels: orchestrator (Dhanaraj and Parkhe, 2006); facilitator (McEvily and Zaheer, 2004); flagship firm (Rugman and D'Cruz, 2003); focal firm (Capaldo, 2007); hub (Jarillo, 1988); or triggering entity (Doz et al., 2000). Since a lead organization is claimed to have a significant impact on innovation network performance, a description of its roles is needed. Our study of the Polish Aviation Valley Association (AVA) aims at elucidating the roles played in the network and network-oriented processes carried out by leading organizations which together define network leadership.

This chapter is organized in four sections, followed by conclusions and limitations. In the first section we review the literature on innovative network leadership, focusing on its scope and functions. The second section explains the empirical research design. We have adopted a qualitative perspective, applying a case study approach both to test prior theoretical propositions and to build network leadership theory. The third section displays our empirical results, ordered along an event story and according to a qualitative comparative analysis framework. The fourth section discusses the empirical results and contains some propositions as to network leadership emerging theory.

Theoretical Underpinnings

Networks are multifaceted and heterogeneous phenomena that take diverse forms, have different sizes and range, and display various structural features. Networks are made of members and relationships between them. In most real networks, members play different roles: some are leading, while others remain peripheral. Such networks are categorized as asymmetrical. Their leading members play a crucial role for network performance, development and existence (Lorenzoni and Baden-Fuller, 1995; Hinterhuber, 2002). In cases of innovation networks these leading members are network command centres especially for innovation and knowledge processes taking place inside the network.

Significant diversity and independence of network actors and their focus on individual objectives call for management (Möller and Halinen, 1999; Knight and Harland, 2005; Möller et al., 2005). To ensure a cohesive and efficient network activity, the lead organization displays specific features and plays a significant role in network development and shaping its performance (Czakon and Klimas, 2011). From the standpoint of a network leader's specific attributes and features the literature suggests that it can be identified against reputation (Wolfe and Gertler, 2004; Niosi and Zhegu, 2005); position (Jarillo, 1988; McEvily and Zaheer, 2004); size (Markusen, 1996; Agrawal and Cockburn, 2003; Dembinski, 2009); and power (Doz et al., 2000; Sabatier et al., 2010) criteria. These attributes yield a very wide category of organizations, which can influence other firms in networks. These criteria are actually factors of network power, yet they do not provide any indication of why some firms choose to use their potential while others do not. Also, the process of influencing the network remains out of focus in this approach.

NETWORK LEADERSHIP SCOPE

The features and activities of leading organizations have been under scrutiny from several standpoints, levels of analysis and methodologies. Consequently, scholars have introduced different labels for the leading organization and identified a wide variety of actions, processes and features carried out by innovation network leaders.

Along with the growing interest in alliances and networks, the idea of distinctive roles played by some actors has been introduced. The innovation network literature allows us to identify four popular but different labels for the leading role: focal firm, facilitator, hub and orchestrator. A *focal firm* is a typical term used in the field of supply chains (Hinterhuber, 2002; Chun-Der et al., 2009; Dembinski, 2009) and innovation networks (Capaldo, 2007). Focal firms coordinate innovation networks, especially through relationship building (Capaldo, 2007), which allows knowledge creation and distribution within the network (Chun-Der et al., 2009; Dembinski, 2009). From the perspective of innovation network performance the focal firm influences the knowledge processes by engaging in intra-network communication processes.

A *facilitator* concentrates on gaining external knowledge, available outside the network and funnelling it inside (Yokakul and Zawdie, 2010). Hence, a facilitator coordinates knowledge spreading and exploitation within the network. A strong orientation on capturing external knowledge contributes to increasing the network's innovativeness and performance. Prior research indicates that network facilitators should be able to stimulate intra-network trust (McEvily and Zaheer, 2004). The role of reciprocal trust creator carried out among network members accelerates learning processes and facilitates knowledge sharing (Yokakul and Zawdie, 2010). This type of leading organization is identified within innovation (Yokakul and Zawdie, 2010) and horizontal networks (McEvily and Zaheer, 2004).

The *hub firm* is a key actor identified inside asymmetric strategic (Jarillo, 1988) and innovation (Dhanaraj and Parkhe, 2006) networks, as well as within value chains (Sabatier et al., 2010) and industrial districts (Markusen, 1996). This type of leading organization takes proactive care of the whole network, ensuring appropriate levels of coordination and integration.

Table 9.1   Features and functions of a network-leading entity

Theoretical perspective	Author	Lead organization	Focus	Features and activities
Innovation networks	Capaldo (2007)	Focal firm	Knowledge management and ability to build relationships	A focal firm should maximize the proportion of bridges to total contacts in the network. It should focus on the diversity of its direct contacts to increase potential to generate innovation.
	Yokakul and Zawdie (2010)	Network facilitator	Knowledge management and social embeddedness	It promotes the development of entrepreneurship and social capital in the community. It acts as "gatekeeper", acquiring knowledge from outside the community and making it accessible for members to use and engage in knowledge-sharing and exchange. The aim is to build a culture of trust to stimulate interactive learning, creativity and innovation within the evolving social network.
	Dhanaraj and Parkhe (2006)	Orchestrator	Ability to leverage innovativeness	Special type of hub firm which manages knowledge mobility, innovation appropriability and network stability. All these activities contribute to the increase of innovation output.
	Dhanaraj and Parkhe (2006)	Hub firm	Ability to orchestrate	It possesses prominence and power gained through individual attributes and a central position in the network structure; performs a leadership role in pulling together the dispersed resources and capabilities of network members.

The *network orchestrator* (Dhanaraj and Parkhe, 2006) is a specific hub firm which runs innovation networks. Empirical research suggests that network orchestrators play a set of roles and a variety of processes labelled orchestration (Möller et al., 2002) – see Table 9.1 above.

Primarily it frames and manages: (1) knowledge mobility; (2) innovation appropriability; and (3) network stability (Dhanaraj and Parkhe, 2006).

Moreover, the network orchestrator integrates networks by setting network strategy and whole sets of procedures, norms and standards of the network (Sabatier et al., 2010). The concept has been further extended to include two more processes: innovation initiation and innovation process management (Batterink et al., 2010). The orchestration role can be played by a hub firm (Dhanaraj and Parkhe, 2006), a focal firm (Hinterhuber, 2002), innovation brokers (Batterink et al., 2010) or by dedicated coordinating firms (Sabatier et al., 2010). Extant literature identifies a variety of other leading organization characteristics for other types of networked cooperative processes. From a regional level of analysis, the concept of *anchor tenant* (Markusen, 1996; Agrawal and Cockburn, 2003; Wolfe and Gertler, 2004; Niosi and Zhegu, 2005) has been introduced in order to elucidate the distinctive roles played by actors in regional innovation systems. Another type of network leader, responsible for collaboration initiating, is called *triggering entity*. It prepares grounds for R&D cooperation (Doz and Baburoglu, 2000; Doz et al., 2000). Last but not least, the *flagship firm* is characterized by: (1) multinational operations and (2) tight network operations within networks co-created by leading providers, clients, competitors and non-business infrastructures (Rugman and D'Cruz, 2003).

All in all, the labels used, as well as the structure and scope of the orchestration processes, seem dependent on the network's type in focus. Yet, prior research identifies a wide variety of leading roles, of different scopes, and incoherent empirical findings. For instance, the most similar concepts measured by similarities in features are focal firm and network facilitator; and focal firm and orchestrator – the latter displaying a clearly broadest scope. On the other hand, the most specific concepts measured by distinct features are the anchor firm and the triggering entity. Therefore, our understanding of the network leadership concept appears at least as fragmented, if not blurry.

NETWORK LEADERSHIP FUNCTIONS

Previous network leaders' scrutiny has shed light on a list of empirically grounded features. The literature suggests that if a firm displays network leader features, then it is a network leader. However, the features do not unveil the complex nature of leadership itself. To ensure a competitive advantage of the network the leader should concentrate on (1) network coordination and development; (2) knowledge and innovation management; and (3) relationship management (see Table 9.2 on the following page).

Table 9.2   Components of a network key actor's role

Component	Feature, attribute, function	Authors
Network coordination and development	1. Setting strategy	Lorenzoni and Baden-Fuller (1995) Hinterhuber (2002) Dhanaraj and Parkhe (2006) Sabatier et al. (2010)
	2. Setting up the network	Jarillo (1988) Doz et al. (2000) Dhanaraj and Parkhe (2006)
	3. Attracting partners	Agrawal and Cockburn (2003) Wolfe and Gertler (2004) Niosi and Zhegu (2005)
	4. Selecting appropriate partners	Lorenzoni and Baden-Fuller (1995) Agrawal and Cockburn (2003) Wolfe and Gertler (2004) Niosi and Zhegu (2005)
	5. Integration	Lorenzoni and Baden-Fuller (1995) Hinterhuber (2002) McEvily and Zaheer (2004) Dhanaraj and Parkhe (2006) Chun-Der et al. (2009) Sabatier et al. (2010)
	6. Coordination	Lorenzoni and Baden-Fuller (1995) McEvily and Zaheer (2004) Chun-Der et al. (2009) Dembinski (2009)
	7. Setting standards and procedures	Lorenzoni and Baden-Fuller (1995) Hinterhuber (2002) Dhanaraj and Parkhe (2006) Sabatier et al. (2010)
	8. Active and permanent care of network activity	Jarillo (1988)
	9. Stability ensuring	Dhanaraj and Parkhe (2006) Sabatier et al. (2010)
Knowledge and innovation management	10. Knowledge providing	Wolfe and Gertler (2004) Niosi and Zhegu (2005) Yokakul and Zawdie (2010)
	11. Knowledge management	Hinterhuber (2002) Wolfe and Gertler (2004) Niosi and Zhegu (2005) Dhanaraj and Parkhe (2006) Capaldo (2007) Chun-Der et al. (2009) Dembinski (2009) Sabatier et al. (2010) Yokakul and Zawdie (2010)

Table 9.2   Continued

Component	Feature, attribute, function	Authors
Knowledge and innovation management (continued)	12. Leveraging innovativeness	Lorenzoni and Baden-Fuller (1995) Hinterhuber (2002) Agrawal and Cockburn (2003) Dhanaraj and Parkhe (2006) Capaldo (2007) Sabatier et al. (2010) Yokakul and Zawdie (2010)
	13. Innovation process management	Sabatier et al. (2010)
	14. R&D initiatives	Agrawal and Cockburn (2003) Niosi and Zhegu (2005)
	15. Value management and rent appropriation	Hinterhuber (2002) Dhanaraj and Parkhe (2006) Dembinski (2009) Sabatier et al. (2010)
Communication and relationship management	16. Relationship building	McEvily and Zaheer (2004) Capaldo (2007) Chun-Der et al. (2009) Yokakul and Zawdie (2010)
	17. Trust generation	Lorenzoni and Baden-Fuller (1995) Doz et al. (2000) McEvily and Zaheer (2004) Yokakul and Zawdie (2010)
	18. Social capital management	Yokakul and Zawdie (2010)
	19. Social embeddedness	Doz et al. (2000) McEvily and Zaheer (2004) Yokakul and Zawdie (2010)
	20. Communication	Reagans and Zuckerman (2001) Cross et al. (2001) Dhanaraj and Parkhe (2006) Prell et al. (2008)

Network coordination and development

Network leading firms are able to coordinate members' actions and integrate the whole network created around them. The leader sets up strategies and development objectives, recruits potential partners and attracts desirable members. It is a sort of command centre in the network and its core. Managing organizations ensure network cohesion and integrity through coordination processes. Inter-organizational networks consist of diversified and independent members. Consistent cooperation requires matching and harmonizing their activities. It is also necessary to fit partners in terms of organizational or social criteria.

Network coordination frames the network's value creation and value distribution processes. Network managers may use three coordination mechanisms: market, hierarchy or social coordination (Jones et al., 1997). Market coordination relies upon prices, formal contracts and bilateral protection within the network. To ensure hierarchical coordination network managers define the network structures, systems of control, rules of organizational integration and bureaucratic allocation of resources. Social coordination is grounded in the setting of social norms and values, inspiring and spreading reciprocal trust – information exchange between members (Joshi and Campbell, 2003). It is important to consider a wide range of methods for improving network coordination – the better coordination, the higher level of network performance.

Knowledge and innovation management

The lead organization initiates, frames, shapes and performs knowledge creation, exchange, transfer and diffusion within the network. It carries out intensive activities in the field of R&D and often commercializes innovations. Processes of spreading knowledge, innovativeness and entrepreneurship require advanced communication and relational skills (Dyer and Singh, 1998). Knowledge and innovation management includes acquiring, making available, spreading and sharing knowledge (Nonaka and Takeuchi, 1995), its transfer and diffusion, and even knowledge-storing processes. The network strategic centre is knowledge and innovation oriented; therefore it often appropriates knowledge rent generated inside the network. Those processes have been found to positively impact development and gain competitive advantage (Grant and Baden-Fuller, 2004; Dhanaraj and Parkhe, 2006), but still there is a gap in our understanding of their trajectories (Østergaard, 2009).

Relationship management

The leading firm organizes the network of partners and takes care of ties and communication channels. Processes of building durable relationships (Capaldo, 2007) are based on stimulating, supporting and reinforcing mutual trust (Gulati et al., 2000; Das and Teng, 2001). Relationship management refers to building, maintaining and reinforcing relationships between members. Moreover, activities related to mediating conflicts arising within the network, building social capital (Balkundi and Kilduff, 2005) and communication management should be undertaken. Communication processes' aim is to share relevant information; therefore it is important for improving network coordination (Reagans and Zuckerman, 2001) and knowledge management. Both internal and external communication significantly facilitates and accelerates knowledge management (Cross et al., 2001; Prell et al., 2008). The implementation of network leadership processes related to communication and relationship management requires a relational capability (Dyer and Singh, 1998; Lorenzoni and Lipparini, 1999; Capaldo, 2007; Czakon, 2009). Moreover, networks consist of autonomous, independent members and a great number of varied, complex relationships which often cannot be fully supervised, or even controlled by a network manager. This might explain why some authors suggest that inter-organizational networks cannot be managed at all (Knight and Harland, 2005).

Our succinct literature review suggests that the network leadership role is far from being untangled. Many concepts of different scope are used, which provide a sound basis for integrative studies. Yet, while the picture of network leadership is relatively advanced, through the available list of roles and processes, our understanding of its dynamics is far less complete.

Research Design

Our study aims at contributing to advanced theory by investigating the features and the processes of innovative network leadership. We adopt a case study approach to investigate an innovative, knowledge-intensive and networked industry in order to improve the understanding of innovation network leadership. To do so, we address a research question: What are the processes implemented by the leader to develop an innovation network in knowledge-intensive industries?

We aim at elucidating the sufficient condition proposition which emerges from prior research investigating the compound nature of the network leadership process. Moreover, prior research applied predominantly a static approach to network leadership, focused on picturing it at a specific point in time. Therefore, we propose to apply a more dynamic approach to leadership, i.e. considering the actions and processes carried out by the leader over time.

METHOD

When the phenomenon under scrutiny is relatively novel to the literature, its boundaries with the business context is unclear (Yin, 1984) and develops in time (Lorenzoni and Lipparini, 1999), the case study method is recommended. We use a case study to build theory.

CASE SELECTION

Theoretical sampling is the cornerstone for case studies as it enables a sharp, clear and in-depth description of the phenomenon under scrutiny. Therefore, case selection needs to be clearly justified. The rationale for selecting the aerospace industry and the Aviation Valley network from it relies on several arguments.

Firstly, the aerospace industry in Poland is the most R&D-intensive, innovative and developmental high-tech and knowledge-intensive industry of the country's economy (Baczko, 2012). The aerospace industry (aviation sector) is seen as knowledge-intensive regarding the OECD high-technology classification (manufacturing industries classified according to their global technological intensity, including ISIC Revision 2 and NACE Revision 1.1) applied, for instance, by Eurostat. Moreover, the aviation sector is included to the High Value Manufacturing Industries counted in knowledge-intensive industries – a classification applied by the UK's Centre for Cities.

Secondly, some aviation players play a role which is far more significant and recognized by others. Size and research intensity coupled with laboratories can reasonably be expected to provide insights into leaders' roles in the industry.

Thirdly, the aerospace industry in Poland is strongly networked. Due to mergers and acquisitions, foreign direct investment projects and extensive privatization conducted for more than a decade, the industry is embedded in the global supply chains. More than that, the industry is, for the most part, located in one region which favours the formation of aviation clusters.

Fourthly, within the aerospace industry in Poland four aviation clusters can be identified. The oldest (established in 2003), the biggest (83 members; 23,000 employees) and the most significant cluster in terms of total turnover (around $1 billion) has been chosen for analysis – the Aviation Valley Association (AVA). Furthermore, the chosen cluster – as one of two Polish aviation clusters – fulfils the definition of an innovative network adopted in this chapter. Additional justification for the deliberate choice of the AVA is the fact that it displays four different localizations, with four large firms operating in each. Size (Agrawal and Cockburn, 2003; Dembinski, 2009) and network centrality (Gnyawali and Madhavan, 2001) are in line with prior research, as key features of a network leader.

DATA COLLECTION

The data were collected between October 2009 and November 2010. We conducted 22 semi-structured interviews with top managers of R&D-intensive AVA members. The questionnaire has been structured around performance, innovation and strategy both at organization and network levels of analysis. A typical interview exceeded two hours, with about one hour consisting of interpretation, discussion and additional issues. The questionnaire was sent to 71 AVA members in March 2010, with a response ratio of 24 per cent, giving a number of valid surveys below the minimum required. Therefore, further contacts, through email (115), telephone (361) and on-site interviews or observation have been used to collect data. We also attended two AVA annual conferences summarizing its activities and the scientific output. The data gathered allowed us to identify the AVA's R&D projects, the roles played by actors and to confront interview findings against other respondents as well as our observations.

Secondary data sources included available publications and literature about the Polish aviation industry and the Aviation Valley Association (newspapers, newsletters, websites, databases, Polish Agency for Foreign Investment reports, AVA's annual statements, AVA members annual statements). These databases have been used to confront our on-site findings as well as to complement datasets on network development.

DATA ANALYSIS

We have used two techniques of organizing the data gathered. Firstly, we have crafted an event story (Langley, 1999), describing key events in AVA development which cover network development of the industry. This technique shows both the process milestones and the role played by actors from the AVA's inception up to the current period. Secondly, we have used Qualitative Comparative Analysis (Kogut and Ragin, 2006). Given the objectives of our study, we have limited the technique to comparing the roles of all key players in the industry with the functions identified in the literature.

Results

In the Aviation Valley four locations can be identified:

1. Bielsko-Biała, consisting of 11 members, including Avio Polska as potential leader;

2. Rzeszów, consisting of 53 members, with WSK Rzeszów as potential leader;

3. Mielec, consisting of 11 members, with PZL Mielec as potential leader;

4. Świdnik, consisting of four members, with PZL Świdnik as potential leader.

These four companies have displayed features necessary to act as network leader and to shape the cluster's performance and innovativeness. All of them are large and reputable companies, their investments and activity shaping the Polish aviation industry (Polish Agency for Enterprise Development/PARP; Baczko, 2012). However, interviews showed that only one of them has decided to undertake the role of a leading organization.

THE AVIATION VALLEY ASSOCIATION: NETWORK DEVELOPMENT

The Aviation Valley Association was registered on 6 November 2003, which can be considered as the formal inception date of the aviation industry network.

In 2003, a small group of engineers envisaged creating Aviation Valley – a centre of the Central European aviation industry. The establishment of the AVA would have been impossible without financial support provided by WSK Rzeszów. The transfer of €250,000 significantly facilitated the first network's initiatives. Furthermore, at the beginning of its operations the office of the AVA was located in WSK Rzeszów's headquarters. The strategic objectives of the Aviation Valley development coincided with the cooperation needs of WSK Rzeszów. At the first general meeting a board was elected and WSK Rzeszów's CEO has been AVA president ever since. Strategic decisions are made by the board and its president, which makes the AVA and WSK Rzeszów interlocked.

Moreover, the founding, organizing and managing activities were undertaken by WSK Rzeszów before formal cluster establishment. In spite of other large and reputable firms being able to fulfil the strategic central role, no other organization has shown such intentions. PZL Świdnik has founded a "mini cluster" together with Lublin University of Technology and participates more in international projects than in AVA initiatives: "we are a little bit on the edge of the Valley [...] we do not have the material advantages, in case of projects we prefer cooperate internationally" (R&D manager, PZL Świdnik). Avio Polska has its own cluster too. The Silesian Aviation Cluster has been

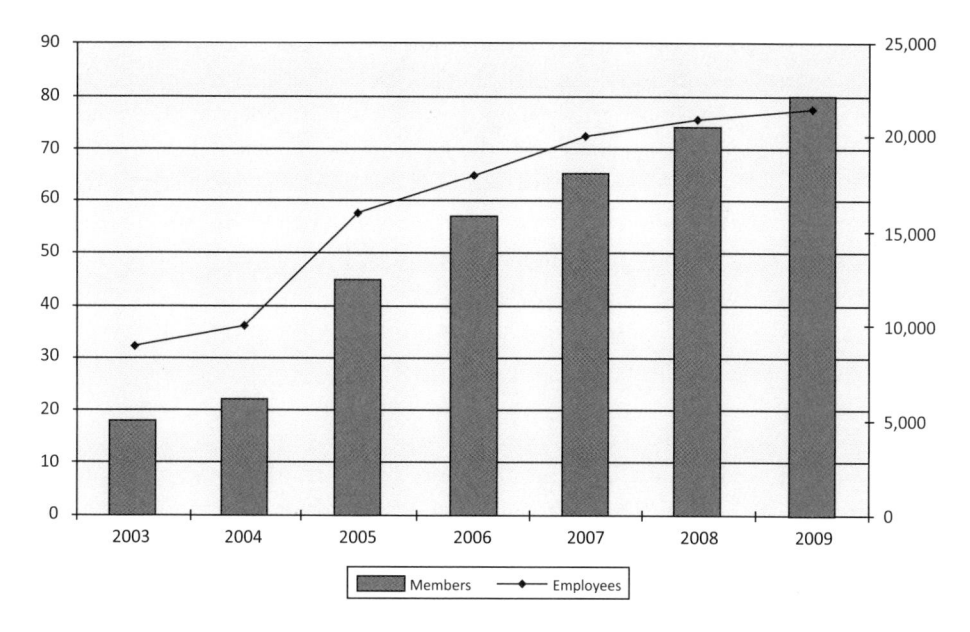

Figure 9.1   Aviation Valley Association network growth

created around the firm: "We are everything in the cluster, we manage all this", said the Director of Development at Avio Polska. The only one exception is PZL Mielec, which is still firmly rooted in Aviation Valley and collaborates closely with its members. But note that PZL Mielec is owned by United Technologies Corporation (UTC), just like WSK Rzeszów.

Initially, every Polish company from the aviation industry could become a network participant. Candidate members currently have to be located in southeastern Poland, be related to the aviation or aerospace industry and should have recommendation from two AVA members – which suggests concerns about network cohesion. The network's growth is shown in Figure 9.1 above.

On the other hand, the AVA president made efforts to attract new "appropriate and desirable" members to the network. High activity in the global aviation industry contributed to the increase of the cluster's familiarity, international connections and building global prestige.

Between 2003 and 2005 a new process in the AVA network emerges, namely inward-oriented networking. Aviation Valley organized a set of reciprocal visits. WSK Rzeszów coordinates and integrates the whole network. Under WSK's patronage, the meetings of the members, conferences and study visits are organized. To ensure closer collaboration and greater network cohesion the AVA board has initiated the mutual benchmarking visits programme (later expanded to foreign, non-participating companies). Members visited several plants and companies associated with the network, and collected information, knowledge and common experiences. A benchmarking programme contributes to mutual acquainting, matching potential business partners, mutual learning, harmonizing and improving members' activities. But, above all, study visits improved coordination and knowledge exchange on issues of common concern, mostly on applied solutions and technologies. Aviation Valley consists of a variety of relationships.

WSK Rzeszów plays an important role in maintaining relationships mainly by stimulation, supporting and reinforcing mutual and multilateral commitment and trust. The CEO strongly emphasizes shared values and passion during meetings, conferences or workshops. Furthermore, he still highlights the value of small and medium businesses/enterprises (SMEs) for cluster activity: "All [the] Valley and our future rely on small, family business [...] our strength lies in small firms together we will create a Polish plane". The significant components of relationship management within Aviation Valley are strong and deeply embedded informal relations and contact between top managers and owners of SMEs. Most of them know each other from engineering classes at the Rzeszów University of Technology. They are connected by long-term cooperation, joint passion and friendship.

From 2006 until now another process has been launched, focused expressly on research, development and innovation. Generally speaking, since 2006 AVA policy has been oriented on the development and strengthening of internal cooperation processes. It is based on long-term contracts for subcontracting or for providing services and joint participation in research projects related to a wide range of knowledge processes (Table 9.3). The majority of the knowledge-creation, acquisition, exchange, transfer and diffusion processes are realized through joint projects, often co-financed by the European Union (EU) or the Polish government. The total value of AVA projects in the knowledge management field tops €155 million, making the aviation industry the primary beneficiary of public research funding in Poland.

An interesting initiative related to the network knowledge management is the AERONET (AErosol RObotic NETwork) project. AERONET, started in 2004 is a project of R&D collaboration intended for universities of technology, aviation companies and institutions. AERONET has allowed Polish aviation organizations to coordinate their individual efforts in the field

Table 9.3   Projects conducted via Aviation Valley

Project	Value (€)	Time frame
INTERREG IIIA – Development and promotion of cross-border Polish–Ukrainian aviation cluster	132,000	2004–2006
Foresight – Directions in development of material technologies for the Aviation Valley cluster	75,000	2006–2008
Integrated Operational Regional Development Programme – Joint Sky – development and integration of the innovating aviation cluster	160,000	2007–2013
Industry contact point	100,000	2007–2013
Podkarpackie Science and Technology Park Aeropolis	12,000,000	2007
Aviation Valley Laboratory	9,000,000	2007
CEKSO – Regional Centre for Transfer of Modern Technology	90,000,000	2007
Enterprise Europe Network	167,000	2008–2011
Wings for Regions – under Competitiveness and Innovation Framework Programme	150,000	2009–2011
Research and Development Center for Aerospace Propulsion	44,000,000	2009

of R&D, specifically designing aeronautical structures and aircraft engines; and improvement of avionics systems, materials engineering and processing in the aeronautical industry. Only 16 AVA members participate in AERONET. The strongest commitment is displayed by Rzeszów University of Technology (project coordinator) and WSK Rzeszów (they are the core of the project, participating in most of the sub-projects). To conclude, AERONET gives its participants access to expertise, tacit knowledge, latest research results and state-of-the-art technology.

Knowledge diffusion within the network runs mainly by benchmarking visits, training or (work, business and general) meetings. All these forms of knowledge transfer are supported by WSK Rzeszów's CEO, who said: "Knowledge and continuous education is a foundation of our development". Furthermore, WSK Rzeszów delegates its own staff and engineers to subcontractors and suppliers, and organizes workshop for partner employees. In-house training provided by WSK Rzeszów's employees is oriented on teaching partners in how to apply new technologies, how to use and operate machinery and how to meet standards and requirements.

From 2008 until now, a fourth process has been launched in the AVA network, which is external networking aimed at increasing commercial ties of the AVA in the global market. In order to achieve this, a number of initiatives – international fair attendance, conferences etc. – have been completed. In May 2010 the AVA organized its first Aviation Valley Expo Day and B2B Meeting. The fair was attended by 60 exhibitors and 300 visitors from all over the world (Japan, the USA, Canada, Finland, Germany and Slovakia). The main objective of the meeting was to gather industry professionals for direct talks with several dozen Polish aerospace companies, members of Aviation Valley.

NETWORK KEY ROLES

An overview of the literature provides a list of activities and functions which can characterize the strategic network centre (see Table 9.2). Based on gathered data and conducted interviews we received output information presented in Table 9.4 below.

Table 9.4   Functions of the AVA's key actors

Features and activities	Avio Polska	WSK Rzeszów	PZL Mielec	PZL Świdnik
1. Able to create strong and bridging relationships	✓	✓	✗	✗
2. Attracts desirable organizations	✓	✓	✓	✗
3. Builds mutual trust and engagement	✗	✓	✗	✗
4. Coordinates	✗	✓	✓	✓
5. Creates vision	✓	✓	✓	✓
6. Decides about system development (sets strategy, procedures and standards)	✓	✓	✓	✗
7. Develops concepts and commercializes innovations	✓	✓	✓	✓
8. Enhances the regional innovation system	✓	✓	✓	✓
9. Ensures network stability	✗	✓	✗	✗
10. Expects creativity	✓	✓	✓	✓
11. Expects sharing knowledge	✓	✓	✓	✗
12. Integrates partners' activities	✓	✓	✓	✓
13. Leverages network innovativeness	✓	✓	✓	✓
14. Management centre	✗	✓	✗	✗
15. Manages knowledge in network	✓	✓	✗	✗
16. Protects innovations	✓	✓	✓	✓
17. Provides knowledge	✓	✓	✓	✓
18. Provides original components and elements	✓	✓	✓	✓
19. Selects appropriate partners (runs recruitment)	✗	✓	✓	✓
20. Sets up network	✗	✓	✗	✗
21. Value creator	✓	✓	✓	✓
Total	15	21	15	12

The biggest number of leading organization functions characterizes WSK Rzeszów. Within the network's leader roles distinctive for WSK Rzeszów there are: (3) building network trust and commitment; (9) ensuring network stability; (14) managing the network as a strategic core; and (20) setting up the network. It should be emphasized that none of other potential leaders performs the above functions. In other words, only WSK Rzeszów has covered the full scope of network leadership processes. However, there are some important facts and aspects of its activity which can determine that it is the most significant and influential organization in the whole network. It is an extremely large company with high potential and financial support provided by UTC. It also has large resources of knowledge, information, experience and connections created and generated for over 80 years.

Discussion

In the case of Aviation Valley roles related to coordination, knowledge and innovation management, and communication and relationship management are played by one actor. WSK Rzeszów appears as the originator, coordinator or at least as a participant in developmental research projects implemented by Aviation Valley. Its deliberate efforts in this field provide significant benefits: public financing, cost-sharing, access to knowledge, supplier networks formation, access to complementary skills and resources. Empirical data suggest that there are four candidates with very similar network power in the AVA. According to prior literature all of them should become network leaders. The conducted qualitative comparative analysis suggests that while active in the R&D field, three actors did not commit to network coordination initiatives. Despite sufficient potential, they opted for other roles and strategic choices. This allows us to formulate the following propositions.

PROPOSITION I: NETWORK LEADERSHIP IS A DELIBERATE STRATEGY, NOT A FUNCTION OF ATTRIBUTES OR A PHENOMENON

We believe that this finding brings a substantial contribution to the literature. Prior research focused extensively on network leader attributes, generating a list of factors which provide power in the network. Our case suggests that power is a potential which can be used or not. This implies that extant propositions suggesting that if a network member is powerful then it is a leader (Agrawal and Cockburn, 2003; Dhanaraj and Parkhe, 2006) have to be rejected. Out of four powerful firms, two of them being final product manufacturers, only one – a second-tier supplier – took the lead of the Aviation Valley Association.

Interestingly, the comparative qualitative analysis allowed us also to validate a tool for identifying network leaders. From the three potential leaders, each dropped commitments to network coordination. Those firms remain knowledge intensive and relationally capable, but do not display any interest in taking charge of network coordination. Specifically, they did not intentionally commit to setting up the network, ensuring its stability, building trust and being a management centre. Inversely, WSK Rzeszów has taken up this challenge, and is strongly committed to the creation of a formal institution. While there is a clear director interlock between the AVA and WSK Rzeszów, the network leader, current activities connected to network coordination have been delegated to an institution created on purpose. This allows the articulation of the second proposition.

PROPOSITION 2: NETWORK MANAGEMENT WITHIN NETWORK LEADERSHIP IS A SEPARATE FUNCTION, WHICH CAN BE DELEGATED AS SUCH TO A SPECIALIZED UNIT

Our study provides evidence that innovation network leadership is composed of three processes, focusing on networks, knowledge and relationships. The network coordination process in the AVA has been appropriated before the formal network foundation. Firstly, WSK Rzeszów coordinates the network and manages its development by:

1. strong commitment in the implementation of development projects;

2. creating demand for products and services supplied by members of the AVA;

3. attracting potential foreign partners;

4. significant cooperative activity at national, regional, international and global levels;

5. strong and personal commitment to AVA activity.

Secondly, managing an entity ensures knowledge transfer and innovation diffusion by:

1. orientation on knowledge sharing (mainly) with subcontractors (mostly SMEs);

2. providing the latest, most desirable and appropriate world-class technologies and high-technology machines, devices and tools;

3. technological support for cluster members (giving instructions and assistance during production processes and production management);

4. participating in building up qualified natural resources (students, other members' employees);

5. orientation on continuous improvement;

6. location in the global supply chain.

Thirdly, WSK Rzeszów takes care of relationships and communication between network members by:

1. strong and personal commitment to AVA activity;

2. aviation passion of the top management;

3. a large network of national and international contacts (business and personal within the industry);

4. strong informal relationships with others crucial cluster players.

PROPOSITION 3: NETWORK ORCHESTRATION INVOLVES THREE CORE PROCESSES – NETWORK COORDINATION, KNOWLEDGE MANAGEMENT AND RELATIONSHIP MANAGEMENT

Our evidence suggests that three processes make up network leadership, which is consistent with extant literature (Dhanaraj and Parkhe, 2006). However, our evidence complements the scope of prior orchestration processes' definition. Network coordination has been vastly missing from prior frameworks, whether understood as network governance or more specifically oriented on formal procedures, contracts and trust-building. Our study brings about evidence of the crucial role played by: trust and trust-building, referrals and reputation, which matches with the social coordination mechanism; procedures and formal coordination referring to bureaucracy; formal contracts and supplier relationships referring to the market mechanism (Jones et al., 1997). Therefore, network stability offers a narrow view of the array of functions actually played by the network leader in the process of coordinating the network.

Summary and Limitations

Innovation becomes increasingly a collective game: very few firms are willing to take the whole risk, are ready to fully fund research and are able to implement innovations all alone. Innovative networks attract increasing attention of researchers. Some innovative networks are successful, while others are not; yet the roles played by actors has so far been under-researched. Particularly, network leadership has been out of focus until relatively recent studies, dating back no more than a decade. Researchers provided both insights into its attributes and some labels – orchestrator, hub, facilitator etc. – depending on the scope of function the actor was in charge of. The need to better understand this role has been confirmed in our literature review, which reveals overlaps in scope, gaps in understanding and a broad omission of process focus. Our study of the Polish Aviation Valley Association suggests that, beyond the capacity to take the lead, a strategic intent makes the difference.

We believe that our study contributes to the theory fivefold. Firstly, we provide a literature review focused on leadership roles, comparing the scope and levels of analysis of the most often used terms: hub, focal firm, facilitator, orchestrator. By doing so, we have been able to identify a list of functions of leaders in different types of innovation networks. This shows how much overlap yet distinctions those concepts revealed, calling for an integrative effort.

Secondly, we have contributed in methodological terms to validating the list of leadership sub-processes as a tool which identifies the leader and rejects potential leaders. Our case offers the opportunity to study the leadership role having four clear candidates, with only one confirmed leader.

Thirdly, we have been able to test a sufficient condition proposition arising from innovative network literature. It suggested that if an organization has the reputation, position, size and resulting power, then it will become a network leader. Well, not really. The missing factor we identified is strategic intent to play this role, and the skills to carry it out.

Fourthly, our findings suggest that a definition of the leader by its features may be misleading. It would call for identifying how a firm's potential can be used. Network leadership was revealed to be a process composed of three distinctive building blocks: network coordination, knowledge management and relationship management. This extends existing literature by adding new elements to the scope of extant network leadership. Moreover, the empirical results show a better understanding of network leadership, which remains one of core processes in the inter-organizational field of inquiry, and it impacts innovation and rent generation. However, these three roles constituting network leadership differ in terms of importance for innovation network performance. The function labelled *knowledge and innovation management* seems to be the priority as it directly affects the efficiency and performance of the innovation network. Meanwhile the other two – i.e. *network coordination and development* and *communication and relationship management* – seem to have an indirect effect on the knowledge-intensive processes shaping innovation network performance. This indicates the processes which should attract the greatest attention of the core organizations in innovation networks.

Fifthly, our study unveils the dynamics of leadership, showing how the leader behaves over time. It indeed requires initial triggering commitment and actions, then strategizing to provide a clear line of action and strong research and development activities, topped by a close look at commercial development.

The limitations of our study come mostly from the method adopted. We are aware that the literature review is succinct and that more publications could have been included in the sample. Also, the literature review could be more systematic in terms of the initial database selection. However, we believe that the selectiveness does not bring significant omission bias into the study. Second, case studies are often seen as low-rigour, third best choice methods. We do not share this overly critical standpoint. However, we believe that the case study procedure needs to be rigorous in its crucial stages: sample selection, data collection and data analysis. The Aviation Valley case study provides opportunities to study an innovation network and reject hypotheses on network leaders. Our data have been triangulated and used to generate an event story which follows a chronological order and a matrix of attributes, which allows a comparative effort.

While the rejection of tested hypothesis is firm, the propositions generated require further investigation. We believe, in particular, that a separate study of network leadership processes holds the promise of rich insights into the phenomenon. An interesting question to explore would be whether each of the three processes can be carried out by another organization.

References

Agrawal, A. and Cockburn, I. (2003). The anchor tenant hypothesis: Exploring the role of large, local, R&D-intensive firms in regional innovation systems. *International Journal of Industrial Organization*, 21, 1227–53.

Baczko, T. (ed.) (2012). *Raport o innowacyjności sektora lotniczego w Polsce w 2010 roku*. Warsaw: Instytut Nauk Ekonomicznych Polskiej Akademii Nauk; Wydawnictwo Key Text.

Balkundi, P. and Kilduff, M. (2005). The ties that lead: A social network approach to leadership. *Leadership Quarterly*, 16, 941–61.

Batterink, M.H., Wubben, E.F.M., Klerkx, L. and Omtaa S.W.F. (2010). Orchestrating innovation networks: The case of innovation brokers in the agri-food sector. *Entrepreneurship and Regional Development*, 22, 47–76.

Capaldo, A. (2007). Network structure and innovation: The leveraging of a dual network as a distinctive relational capability. *Strategic Management Journal*, 28, 585–608.

Chun-Der, Ch., Yi-Wen, F., and Cheng-Kiang, F. (2009). Cultivating focal firm's integration capabilities: Critical determinants supply chain process the investigation of and consequences. *Proceedings of World Academy of Science: Engineering and Technology*, 53, 191–8.

Cross, R., Parker, A., Prusak, L., and Borgatti, S.P. (2001). Knowing what we know: Supporting knowledge creation and sharing in social networks. *Organizational Dynamics*, 30, 100–120.

Czakon, W. (2009). The building blocks of a relational capability: Evidence from the banking industry. *International Journal of Entrepreneurial Venturing*, 1, 131–46.

Czakon, W., and Klimas, P. (2011). *Anchoring and the Orchestration Processes: the Case of Aviation Valley*. In S. Lachiewicz and A. Zakrzewska-Bielawska (eds), *Fundamentals of Management in Modern Small and Medium-Sized Enterprises*. Łódź: Technical University of Lodz Press.

Das, T.K., and Teng, B.S. (2001). Trust, control, and risk in strategic alliances: An integrated framework. *Organization Studies*, 22, 251–83.

Dembinski, P.H. (2009). Very large enterprises, focal firms and global value chains. *Revista de Economía Mundial*, 23, 107–29.

Dhanaraj, C., and Parkhe, A. (2006). Orchestrating innovation networks. *Academy of Management Review*, 31, 659–69.

Doz, Y.L., and Baburoglu, O. (2000). From competition to collaboration: The emergence and evolution of R&D cooperatives. In D. Faulkner and M. de Rond (eds), *Cooperative Strategy: Economic, Business and Organizational Issues*. Oxford: Oxford University Press.

Doz, Y.L., Olk, P.M., and Ring, P.S. (2000). Formation processes of R&D consortia: Which path to take? Where does it lead? *Strategic Management Journal*, 21, 239–66.

Dul, J., and Hak, T. (2008). *Case Study Methodology in Business Research*. Amsterdam: Butterworth-Heinemann.

Dyer, J., and Singh, H. (1998). The relational view: Cooperative strategy and sources of interorganizational competitive advantage. *Academy of Management Review*, 24, 660–79.

Gnyawali, D.R., and Madhavan, R. (2001). Cooperative networks and competitive dynamics: A structural embeddedness perspective. *Academy of Management Review*, 26, 431–45.

Grant, R., and Baden-Fuller, Ch. (2004). A knowledge accessing theory of strategic alliances. *Journal of Management Studies*, 41, 61–84.

Gulati, R., Nohira, N., and Zaheer, A. (2000). Strategic networks. *Strategic Management Journal*, 21, 203–15.

Hagedoorn, J. (1993). Understanding the rationale of strategic technology partnering: Interorganizational modes of cooperation and sectoral differences. *Strategic Management Journal*, 14(5), 371–85.

Häcki, R., and Lighton, J. (2001). The future of the networked company. *McKinsey Quarterly*, 3, 26–39.

Hinterhuber, A. (2002). Value chain orchestration in action and the case of the global agrochemical industry. *Long Range Planning*, 35, 615–35.

Jarillo, J.C. (1988). On strategic networks. *Strategic Management Journal*, 9, 31–41.

Jones, C., Hesterly, W.S., and Borgatti, S.P. (1997). A general theory of network governance: Exchange conditions and social mechanisms. *Academy of Management Review*, 22(4), 911–45.

Joshi, A.W., and Campbell, A.J. (2003). Effect of environmental dynamism on relational governance in manufacturer-supplier relationships: A contingency framework and an empirical test. *Journal of the Academy of Marketing Science*, 31, 176–88.

Kogut, B. (2000). The network as knowledge: Generative rules and the emergence of structure. *Strategic Management Journal*, 21, 405–25.

Kogut, B., and Ragin, C. (2006). Exploring complexity when diversity is limited: Institutional complementarity in theories of rule of law and national systems revisited. *European Management Review*, 3, 44–59.

Knight, L., and Harland, Ch. (2005). Managing supply networks: Organizational roles in network management. *European Management Journal*, 23, 281–92.

Langley, A. (1999). Strategies for theorizing from process data. *Academy of Management Review*, 24(4), 691–710.

Lorenzoni, G., and Baden-Fuller, Ch. (1995). Creating a Strategic center to manage a web of partners. *California Management Review*, 37, 146–63.

Lorenzoni, G., and Lipparini, A. (1999). The leveraging of interfirm relationships as a distinctive organizational capability: A longitudinal study. *Strategic Management Journal*, 20, 317–38.

Majumder, P., and Srinivasan, A. (2008). Leadership and competition in network supply chains. *Management Science*, 54, 1189–204.

Markusen, A. (1996). Sticky places in slippery space: A typology of industrial districts. *Economic Geography*, 72, 293–313.

McEvily, B., and Zaheer, A. (2004). Architects of trust: The role of network facilitators in geographical clusters. In R.M. Kramer and K.S. Cook (eds), *Trust and Distrust in Organizations: Dilemmas and Approaches*. New York: Russell Sage Foundation.

Möller, K.K., and Halinen, A. (1999). Business relationships and networks: Managerial challenge of network era. *Industrial Marketing Management*, 28, 413–27.

Möller, K.K., Rajala, A., and Svahn, S. (2005). Strategic business nets: Their type and management. *Journal of Business Research*, 58, 1274–84.

Möller, K.K., Svahn, S., Rajala, A., and Tuominen, M. (2002). *Network Management as a Set of Dynamic Capabilities*. 18th Annual Industrial Marketing and Purchasing (IMP) Conference, 5–7 September, Dijon.

Niosi, J., and Zhegu, M. (2005). Aerospace clusters: Local or global knowledge spillovers? *Industry and Innovation*, 12, 5–25.

Nonaka, I., and Takeuchi, H. (1995). *The Knowledge-Creating Company: How Japanese Companies Create the Dynamics of Innovation*. New York: Oxford University Press.

Østergaard, Ch. (2009). Knowledge flows through social networks in a cluster: Comparing university and industry links. *Structural Change and Economic Dynamics*, 20, 196–210.

Powell, W.W., Koput, K.W., and Smith-Doerr, L. (1996). Interorganizational collaboration and the locus of innovation: Networks of learning in biotechnology. *Administrative Science Quarterly*, 41, 116–45.

Prell, K., Hubacek, C., Quinn, C., and Reed, M. (2008). Who's in the network? When stakeholders influence data analysis. *Systematic Practice and Action Research*, 21, 443–58.

Reagans, R., and Zuckerman, E.W. (2001). Networks, diversity, and productivity: The social capital of corporate R&D teams. *Organization Science*, 12, 502–17.

Richard, P.J., and Devinney, T.M. (2005). Modular strategies: B2B technology and architectural knowledge. *California Management Review*, 47, 86–113.

Ring, P.S., Doz, Y.L., and Olk, P.M. (2005). Managing formation processes in R&D consortia. *California Management Review*, 47, 137–56.

Rugman, A.M., and D'Cruz, J.R. (2003). *Multinationals as Flagship Firms: Regional Business Networks*. London: Oxford University Press.

Sabatier, V., Mangematin, V., and Rousselle, T. (2010). Orchestrating networks in the biopharmaceutical industry: Small hub firms can do it. *Production Planning and Control*, 21, 218–28.

Wassermann, S., and Faust, K. (1999). *Social Network Analysis: Methods and Applications*. Cambridge: Cambridge University Press.

Wolfe, D.A., and Gertler, M.S. (2004). Clusters from the inside and out: Local dynamics and global linkages. *Urban Studies*, 41, 1071–93.

Yin, R. (1984). *Case Study Research: Design and Methods*. Beverly Hills, CA: Sage.

Yokakul, N., and Zawdie, G. (2010). Innovation network and technological capability development in the Thai SME sector: The case of the Thai dessert industry. *International Journal of Technology Management and Sustainable Development*, 9, 19–36.

Index

accretion, *see* career accretion
actant 43–8
actor 43
actor network theory 42
advising 19–22
advisory role 19–20, 22
angst 11–12, 19, 22
antidote 11–12, 22
archaeologist 14–18
archival data 126–8; *see also* database
archive 13, 20
articulation work 65–6
artificial and human intelligence 112, 125
austerity 11–12, 19, 22
automatic anti-aircraft system 100
Aviation Valley 142, 143–4
    Aviation Valley Association 144–6

barriers to a professional career 14
battlefield assistants 100
Borzestowski, Waszczyk 97, 103, 106
boundaries
    collaboration across 55–78
    framework for knowledge sharing 57
    syntactic, semantic and pragmatic 56–7
Brunel, Isambard Kingdom 35
budget 12, 15, 19

career 11–15, 17–19, 21–2
career accretion 11, 21–2

career progression 11–12, 21
coaching 22
collecting data 126–7, 129–30
collecting and data processing system (CDPS) 105, 106
community 11–13, 17–20, 22
contract culture 12
coordination mechanisms 57, 65
Cubicon 85–9, 92
curator xi, 13–15, 17, 18
cybernetics 100–102, 111

database 113, 129; *see also* knowledge database
    database dump 128
decision support systems 95, 97, 101, 109
dialogue 46
director 18

ecomuseum 13, 19–22
education 20
enemy 102
engineers 36
engineering 55–78
enrolment 44
Ethical Judgment Center 100, 111
ethics and information technology 109
expert systems 98–100
expertise 18

facilitator 19, 135
figurehead 16, 21

Flodden 1513 Ecomuseum 13, 19–22
focal firm 135
focus group 124–6
funding 13, 17–18
fundraising 13, 16, 18, 20

general management 16–17
global financial crisis 11–12
grounded theory 84

heritage manager xi, 11–21
hub firm 135

identity 11, 21, 61–2, 66–70
implementation 36
inference engine 111, 113
innovation network 133
institutionalization 114, 116, 119
interface 13, 75, 115, 127
interessement 44
international assignment 28
    international assignment, educational 29
    International assignment, work 29
interview, method of 120–21, 123–6
    free 124–5
    in-depth 124, 126
    standardized 121, 123–4

job satisfaction 22

knowledge database 99
knowledge management 137–8, 140
knowledge worker 11, 14, 15, 18, 21, 22

Latour, Bruno 42
leader 12–13, 19
leadership 12, 21, 22
legitimacy 18, 21
line manage 11, 15, 22

local authority 13, 16–17, 19–20, 22

manager 11–22
management 13, 15–18, 20, 22
marketing 14, 16, 18, 20–21
marketing professional 14, 16, 18, 21
matrix of transition-probability 107
middle manager 13
Mobilization of Allies 44
Moral Knowledge Expert System (MKES) 97–103
morale 22
multiple professional backgrounds 11, 21–22
museum xi, 12–16, 18, 20–21

natural language processing 98
nepotism 26
    Wasta 26
netnography 114–15, 120, 126, 130
network 134, 141
    network coordination 140
    network development 140, 144–8
    network leadership 133, 135–6, 148–9
    network management 150–51
neural networks 98
non-participant observation 117–19
novelty 57, 71, 73–6

oil and gas production 55–78
    Norway 55–78
orchestrator 136–7, 151
organizational culture 114, 119

participant observation 117–20
partner 12, 20
partnership 12, 17–18, 22
post-fordism 39
post-war relationships 101

practitioner 18
pragmatic 16, 18, 21
problem solving 55, 100–101
problematization 44
production management 36
professional 11–18, 20, 21
professional bodies 14
professional isolation 15
progression, *see* career progression
project 13–15, 17–20
project managers 55–78
project management 13, 15, 20, 38
prosumers 119, 120, 125–6, 129
    prosumer collectivities 115, 124, 126–7, 130
    prosumer communities 113, 115
    prosumer environment 115, 117, 126
    prosumer projects 115, 117, 126
prosumption 127, 129–30; *see also* prosumers
public sector 11–12, 17, 22
purposive device 100

qualitative rersearch 114–17, 120, 128, 130
quantitative research 113–14, 120

relationship management 140
repatriation 28
    repatriation failure 28
research strategies 114, 118, 123–4, 130
resources
    mobilizing 65–7

salary 16–17
Saudization 27–8
school 13
scientific management 39
self-control 100

self-employed 14–15
self-organizing system 101, 107
servomechanism 101–2
skill 20
Socrates' knowledge search 103
specialism 14, 18
sport professional 14, 16, 18
staff 12, 14–15, 19, 21–2
STS (science and technology studies) 42
subsea systems 55–78
symbolic representations 102
syntax 58, 62–5

Taylor, Frederick W. 39
Taylorism 39
temporary 14
third sector 12–13, 17, 19
tourism 20
transhumanism xiii, 109
translation 43
transition 11, 16, 21–2
transition, negative feelings towards 16–17
transition, positive feelings towards 14, 16–18
transition, to knowledge worker 14
transition, to manager of knowledge workers 15–17
trust
    as a coordination mechanism 57
    various types of 66–75
    in relation to power 70–75

virtual team
    communication in 83
    division of tasks
    management 81–4
    trust 83, 91–2
vision 21

volunteer 14

Wikimedia 113, 115, 118, 129
   projects 113, 127–8, 130
   Wikimedia Foundation 113, 122–3
Wikipedia 113–16, 118–19, 121–2
   wikipedists 115, 119, 121–2, 127, 129
   editors 115–16, 122
   newcomers 115
work, negative feelings towards 12, 19, 22
work, positive feelings towards 19–22
worker 11, 21–2
workshop 48

If you have found this book useful you may be interested in other titles from Gower

Assessment Centres and Global Talent Management
Edited by Nigel Povah and George C. Thornton III
Hardback: 978-1-4094-0386-9
e-book PDF: 978-1-4094-0387-6
e-book ePUB: 978-1-4094-5926-2

**New Directions in Organizational Psychology
and Behavioral Medicine**
Edited by Alexander-Stamatios Antoniou and Cary Cooper
Hardback: 978-1-4094-1082-9
e-book PDF: 978-1-4094-1083-6
e-book ePUB: 978-1-4094-6023-7

Beyond Goals
Effective Strategies for Coaching and Mentoring
Edited by Susan David, David Clutterbuck and David Megginson
Hardback: 978-1-4094-1851-1
e-book PDF: 978-1-4094-1852-8
e-book ePUB: 978-1-4724-0167-0

Human Nature
A Guide to Managing Workplace Relations
Greg Clydesdale
Hardback: 978-1-4094-1851-1
e-book PDF: 978-1-4724-1680-3
e-book ePUB: 978-1-4724-1681-0

Smart Working
Creating the Next Wave
Anne Marie McEwan
Hardback: 978-1-4094-0456-9
e-book PDF: 978-1-4094-0457-6
e-book ePUB: 978-1-4094-6014-5

GOWER